# THE NAVIGATOR

**A Navigational Tool
to be used with the Holy Bible**

Information Assembled by

# Rebecca Herrington

ISBN-13: 978-1985784543

ISBN-10 1985784548

Additional copies are made available through:

www.CreateSpace.com

**This book is reverently dedicated to the One and Only Holy God and His Son Jesus Christ.**

# Index

# INTRODUCTION

The lists in this book have been compiled from some of my own favorite Bible stories in the hope that they will help you to navigate through specific portions of the Bible. None of the lists are all inclusive, but they contain many of the most popular Scripture references where you will find amazing insights. I challenge you to search the entire Bible for yourself to find many more pathways of inspiration and knowledge as well as stories of incredible events. Extra space has been inserted after each section, so you can add your own favorite verses.

I hope you enjoy many trips throughout God's Word. May you discover great treasures for helping you to achieve the rich life God created you to live!

# POPULAR PEOPLE AND EVENTS

## ABRAHAM

**Promises to Abram** – Genesis 12:1-9
*2 "I will make you into a great nation, and I will bless you; I will make your name great, and you will be a blessing.3 I will bless those who bless you, and whoever curses you I will curse; and all peoples on earth  will be blessed through you."*

**Abram in Egypt** – Genesis 12:10-20
*10 Now there was a famine in the land, and Abram went down to Egypt to live there for a while because the famine was severe.*

**Abram Inherits Canaan** – Genesis 13:1-18
*12 Abram lived in the land of Canaan... 14 The LORD said to Abram after Lot had parted from him, "Look around from where you are, to the north and south, to the east and west. 15 All the land that you see I will give to you and your offspring forever.*

**Abram and Melchizedek** – Genesis 14:18-24
*18 Then Melchizedek king of Salem brought out bread and wine. He was priest of God Most High, 19 and he blessed Abram, saying, "Blessed be Abram by God Most High, Creator of heaven and earth. 20 And praise be to God Most High, who delivered your enemies into your hand." Then Abram gave him a tenth of everything.*

**God's Covenant with Abram** – Genesis 15:1-21
*5 He took him outside and said, "Look up at the sky and count the stars—if indeed you can count them." Then he said to him, "So shall your offspring be."*

**The Sign of the Covenant** – Genesis 17:1-27
*10 This is my covenant with you and your descendants after you, the covenant you are to keep: Every male among you shall be circumcised. 11 You are to undergo circumcision, and it will be the sign of the covenant between me and you.*

**Promise of a Son** – Genesis 18:1-15

*[10] Then one of them said, "I will surely return to you about this time next year, and Sarah your wife will have a son."*

**Abraham Intercedes for Sodom** – Genesis 18:16-33

*[23] Then Abraham approached him and said: "Will you sweep away the righteous with the wicked? [24] What if there are fifty righteous people in the city? Will you really sweep it away and not spare[a] the place for the sake of the fifty righteous people in it?*

**Abraham & Abimelek** – Genesis 20:1-18

*[9] Then Abimelek called Abraham in and said, "What have you done to us? How have I wronged you that you have brought such great guilt upon me and my kingdom? You have done things to me that should never be done."*

**Isaac Is Born** – Genesis 21:1-7

*[1] Now the LORD was gracious to Sarah as he had said, and the LORD did for Sarah what he had promised. [2] Sarah became pregnant and bore a son to Abraham in his old age, at the very time God had promised him. [3] Abraham gave the name Isaac to the son Sarah bore him.*

**A Covenant with Abimelek** – Genesis 21:22-34

*[22] At that time Abimelek and Phicol the commander of his forces said to Abraham, "God is with you in everything you do. [23] Now swear to me here before God that you will not deal falsely with me or my children or my descendants. Show to me and the country where you now reside as a foreigner the same kindness I have shown to you."*

**Abraham Tested** – Genesis 22:1-19

*[2] Then God said, "Take your son, your only son, whom you love—Isaac—and go to the region of Moriah. Sacrifice him there as a burnt offering on a mountain I will show you."*

**Abraham's Death** – Genesis 25:7-11
*⁷ Abraham lived a hundred and seventy-five years. ⁸ Then Abraham breathed his last and died at a good old age, an old man and full of years; and he was gathered to his people.*

**Abraham Justified by Faith** – Romans 4:1-4
*³ "Abraham believed God, and it was credited to him as righteousness."*

**Faithful Abraham** – Hebrews 11:8-12
*⁸ By faith Abraham, when called to go to a place he would later receive as his inheritance, obeyed and went, even though he did not know where he was going.*

## ADAM

**Life in God's Garden** -  Genesis 2:8-25
*⁸ Now the LORD God had planted a garden in the east, in Eden; and there he put the man he had formed. ⁹ The LORD God made all kinds of trees grow out of the ground—trees that were pleasing to the eye and good for food. In the middle of the garden were the tree of life and the tree of the knowledge of good and evil.*

**The Temptation and Fall of Man** – Genesis 3:1-24
*¹ Now the serpent was more crafty than any of the wild animals the LORD God had made. He said to the woman, "Did God really say, 'You must not eat from any tree in the garden'?"*
*⁶ When the woman saw that the fruit of the tree was good for food and pleasing to the eye, and also desirable for gaining wisdom, she took some and ate it. She also gave some to her husband, who was with her, and he ate it.*

## ARK OF GOD

**The Ark of God Captured** – 1 Samuel 4:1-11
*¹⁰ So the Philistines fought, and the Israelites were defeated and every man fled to his tent. The slaughter was very great; Israel lost thirty thousand foot soldiers. ¹¹ The ark of God was captured*

**The Philistines and the Ark of God** – 1 Samuel 5:1-12
*6 The LORD's hand was heavy on the people of Ashdod and its vicinity; he brought devastation on them and afflicted them with tumors.*

**The Ark Returned to Israel** – 1 Samuel 6:1-19
*1 When the ark of the LORD had been in Philistine territory seven months, 2 the Philistines called for the priests and the diviners and said, "What shall we do with the ark of the LORD? Tell us how we should send it back to its place."*

**The Ark Brought to Jerusalem** – 2 Samuel 6:1 – 7:1
*3 They set the ark of God on a new cart and brought it from the house of Abinadab, which was on the hill. Uzzah and Ahio, sons of Abinadab, were guiding the new cart 4 with the ark of God on it, and Ahio was walking in front of it. 5 David and all Israel were celebrating with all their might before the LORD, with castanets, harps, lyres, timbrels, sistrums and cymbals.*

## BALAAM

**Balaam, the Donkey & the Angel** – Numbers 22:22-40
*28 Then the LORD opened the donkey's mouth, and it said to Balaam, "What have I done to you to make you beat me these three times?"*

## CREATION

**The History of Creation** – Genesis 1:1 – 2:7
*1 In the beginning God created the heavens and the earth.*

**God's Covenant with Creation** – Genesis 8:20-22
*20 Then Noah built an altar to the LORD and, taking some of all the clean animals and clean birds, he sacrificed burnt offerings on it. 21 The LORD smelled the pleasing aroma and said in his heart: "Never again will I curse the ground because of humans, even though[a] every inclination of the human heart is evil from childhood. And never again will I destroy all living creatures, as I have done. 22 "As long as the earth endures,*

*seedtime and harvest, cold and heat, summer and winter, day
and night will never cease."*

**The Glory of the Lord in Creation** – Psalm 8:1-9
*³ When I consider your heavens, the work of your fingers, the
moon and the stars, which you have set in place, ⁴ what is
mankind that you are mindful of them, human beings that you
care for them?*

**The Sovereignty of the Lord in Creation** – Psalm 33:1-22
*⁶ By the word of the LORD the heavens were made, their starry
host by the breath of his mouth. ⁷ He gathers the waters of the sea
into jars; he puts the deep into storehouses. ⁸ Let all the earth
fear the LORD; let all the people of the world revere him. ⁹ For he
spoke, and it came to be; he commanded, and it stood firm.*

**Praise to the Sovereign Lord for His Creation** – Psalm 104:1-35
*⁵ He set the earth on its foundations; it can never be moved. ⁶ You
covered it with the watery depths as with a garment; the waters
stood above the mountains. ⁷ But at your rebuke the waters fled, at the
sound of your thunder they took to flight; ⁸ they flowed over the
mountains, they went down into the valleys, to the place you
assigned for them. ⁹ You set a boundary they cannot cross; never again
will they cover the earth.*

**Praise to God in Creation and Redemption** – Psalm 135:1-21
*⁵ I know that the LORD is great, that our Lord is greater than all
gods. ⁶ The LORD does whatever pleases him, in the heavens and on the
earth, in the seas and all their depths. ⁷ He makes clouds rise from the
ends of the earth; he sends lightning with the rain and brings out the
wind from his storehouses.*

**Praise to the Lord from Creation** – Psalm 148:1-14
*¹³ Let them praise the name of the LORD, for his name alone is
exalted; his splendor is above the earth and the heavens.*

**The Glorious New Creation** – Isaiah 65:17-25
*¹⁷ "See, I will create new heavens and a new earth. The former things
will not be remembered, nor will they come to mind."*

# DANIEL

**Daniel & His Friends Obey God** – Daniel 1:1-21
*11 Daniel then said to the guard whom the chief official had appointed over Daniel, Hananiah, Mishael and Azariah, 12 "Please test your servants for ten days: Give us nothing but vegetables to eat and water to drink."*

**Daniel's Friends Disobey the King** – Daniel 3:1-18
*12 But there are some Jews whom you have set over the affairs of the province of Babylon—Shadrach, Meshach and Abednego— who pay no attention to you, Your Majesty. They neither serve your gods nor worship the image of gold you have set up."*

**Daniel's Friends Thrown into the Fiery Furnace** – Daniel 3:19-25
*19 Then Nebuchadnezzar was furious with Shadrach, Meshach and Abednego, and his attitude toward them changed. He ordered the furnace heated seven times hotter than usual 20 and commanded some of the strongest soldiers in his army to tie up Shadrach, Meshach and Abednego and throw them into the blazing furnace.*

**The Writing on the Wall** – Daniel 5:1-31
*5 Suddenly the fingers of a human hand appeared and wrote on the plaster of the wall, near the lampstand in the royal palace. The king watched the hand as it wrote.*

**Daniel in the Lion's Den** – Daniel 6:1-28
*16 So the king gave the order, and they brought Daniel and threw him into the lions' den. The king said to Daniel, "May your God, whom you serve continually, rescue you!"*

**Vision of the Four Beasts** – Daniel 7:1-8
*2 Daniel said: "In my vision at night I looked, and there before me were the four winds of heaven churning up the great sea. 3 Four great beasts, each different from the others, came up out of the sea.*

**The Seventy-Weeks Prophecy** – Daniel 9:20-27
*24 "Seventy 'sevens' are decreed for your people and your holy city to finish transgression, to put an end to sin, to atone for wickedness, to bring in everlasting righteousness, to seal up vision and prophecy and to anoint the Most Holy Place."*

**Prophecy of the End Time** – Daniel 12:1-13
*"At that time Michael, the great prince who protects your people, will arise. There will be a time of distress such as has not happened from the beginning of nations until then. But at that time your people—everyone whose name is found written in the book—will be delivered."*

## DAVID

**David Anointed as King** – 1 Samuel 16:1-13
*12 So he sent for him and had him brought in. He was glowing with health and had a fine appearance and handsome features. Then the LORD said, "Rise and anoint him; this is the one."13 So Samuel took the horn of oil and anointed him in the presence of his brothers, and from that day on the Spirit of the LORD came powerfully upon David.*

**David & Goliath** – 1 Samuel 17:1-58
*50 So David triumphed over the Philistine with a sling and a stone; without a sword in his hand he struck down the Philistine and killed him.*

**Saul Resents David** – 1 Samuel 18:1-16
*10 The next day an evil spirit from God came forcefully on Saul. He was prophesying in his house, while David was playing the lyre, as he usually did. Saul had a spear in his hand 11 and he hurled it, saying to himself, "I'll pin David to the wall." But David eluded him twice.*

**Jonathan's Loyalty to David** – 1 Samuel 20:1-42
*4 Jonathan said to David, "Whatever you want me to do, I'll do for you."*

**David Spares Saul's Life** – 1 Samuel 24:1-22
*⁹ He said to Saul, "Why do you listen when men say, 'David is bent on harming you'? ¹⁰ This day you have seen with your own eyes how the LORD delivered you into my hands in the cave. Some urged me to kill you, but I spared you; I said, 'I will not lay my hand on my lord, because he is the LORD's anointed.'"*
1 Samuel 26:1-25
*⁹ But David said to Abishai, "Don't destroy him! Who can lay a hand on the LORD's anointed and be guiltless? ¹⁰ As surely as the LORD lives," he said, "the LORD himself will strike him, or his time will come and he will die, or he will go into battle and perish. ¹¹ But the LORD forbid that I should lay a hand on the LORD's anointed."*

**David Anointed King Over Judah** – 2 Samuel 2:1-7
*⁴ Then the men of Judah came to Hebron, and there they anointed David king over the tribe of Judah.*

**The Ark Brought to Jerusalem** – 2 Samuel 6:1 – 7:1
*³ They set the ark of God on a new cart and brought it from the house of Abinadab, which was on the hill. Uzzah and Ahio, sons of Abinadab, were guiding the new cart ⁴ with the ark of God on it, and Ahio was walking in front of it. ⁵ David and all Israel were celebrating with all their might before the LORD, with castanets,[d] harps, lyres, timbrels, sistrums and cymbals.*

**David & Bathsheba** – 2 Samuel 11:1-27
*² One evening David got up from his bed and walked around on the roof of the palace. From the roof he saw a woman bathing. The woman was very beautiful, ³ and David sent someone to find out about her. The man said, "She is Bathsheba, the daughter of Eliam and the wife of Uriah the Hittite." ⁴ Then David sent messengers to get her. She came to him, and he slept with her.*

**David's Charge to Solomon** – 1 Kings 2:1-12
*² "I am about to go the way of all the earth," he said. "So be strong, act like a man, ³ and observe what the LORD your God requires: Walk in obedience to him, and keep his decrees and commands, his laws and regulations, as written in the Law of*

*Moses. Do this so that you may prosper in all you do and wherever you go ⁴ and that the LORD may keep his promise to me: 'If your descendants watch how they live, and if they walk faithfully before me with all their heart and soul, you will never fail to have a successor on the throne of Israel.'"*

## <u>ELIJAH</u>

**Ravens Feed Elijah** – 1 Kings 17:1-6
*² Then the word of the LORD came to Elijah: ³ "Leave here, turn eastward and hide in the Kerith Ravine, east of the Jordan. ⁴ You will drink from the brook, and I have directed the ravens to supply you with food there."*

**Elijah Saves the Widow of Zarephath** – 1 Kings 17:8-24
*¹³ Elijah said to her, "Don't be afraid. Go home and do as you have said. But first make a small loaf of bread for me from what you have and bring it to me, and then make something for yourself and your son. ¹⁴ For this is what the LORD, the God of Israel, says: 'The jar of flour will not be used up and the jug of oil will not run dry until the day the LORD sends rain on the land.'"*

**Elijah's Proves God is More Powerful than Baal**
    *– 1 Kings 18:20-40*
*³⁸ Then the fire of the LORD fell and burned up the sacrifice, the wood, the stones and the soil, and also licked up the water in the trench. ³⁹ When all the people saw this, they fell prostrate and cried, "The LORD—he is God! The LORD—he is God!"*

**Elijah Escapes from Jezebel** – 1 Kings 19:1-10
*³ Elijah was afraid and ran for his life. When he came to Beersheba in Judah, he left his servant there, ⁴ while he himself went a day's journey into the wilderness. He came to a broom bush, sat down under it and prayed that he might die. "I have had enough, LORD," he said. "Take my life; I am no better than my ancestors." ⁵ Then he lay down under the bush and fell asleep.*

**Elijah Sees the Lord Pass By** – 1 Kings 19:11-18

*11 The LORD said, "Go out and stand on the mountain in the presence of the LORD, for the LORD is about to pass by. "Then a great and powerful wind tore the mountains apart and shattered the rocks before the LORD, but the LORD was not in the wind. After the wind there was an earthquake, but the LORD was not in the earthquake.12 After the earthquake came a fire, but the LORD was not in the fire. And after the fire came a gentle whisper. 13 When Elijah heard it, he pulled his cloak over his face and went out and stood at the mouth of the cave. Then a voice said to him, "What are you doing here, Elijah?"*

**Elijah Ascends to Heaven** – 2 Kings 2:1-18

*11 As they were walking along and talking together, suddenly a chariot of fire and horses of fire appeared and separated the two of them, and Elijah went up to heaven in a whirlwind.*

## ELISHA

**Elisha Calling** – 1 Kings 19:19-21

*19 So Elijah went from there and found Elisha son of Shaphat. He was plowing with twelve yoke of oxen, and he himself was driving the twelfth pair. Elijah went up to him and threw his cloak around him.*

**Elisha and the Widow's Oil** – 2 Kings 4:1-7

*3 Elisha said, "Go around and ask all your neighbors for empty jars. Don't ask for just a few. 4 Then go inside and shut the door behind you and your sons. Pour oil into all the jars, and as each is filled, put it to one side."*

**Elisha Raises the Shunamite's Son** – 2 Kings 4:8-37

*32 When Elisha reached the house, there was the boy lying dead on his couch. 33 He went in, shut the door on the two of them and prayed to the LORD. 34 Then he got on the bed and lay on the boy, mouth to mouth, eyes to eyes, hands to hands. As he stretched himself out on him, the boy's body grew warm. 35 Elisha turned away and walked back and forth in the room and then got*

*on the bed and stretched out on him once more. The boy sneezed
seven times and opened his eyes.*

**Elisha Purifies the Pot of Stew** – 2 Kings 4:38-41
*⁴⁰ The stew was poured out for the men, but as they began to eat
it, they cried out, "Man of God, there is death in the pot!" And
they could not eat it. ⁴¹ Elisha said, "Get some flour." He put it
into the pot and said, "Serve it to the people to eat." And there
was nothing harmful in the pot.*

**Elisha Feeds 100 Men** – 2 Kings 4:42-44
*⁴³ "How can I set this before a hundred men?" his servant asked.
But Elisha answered, "Give it to the people to eat. For this is
what the LORD says: 'They will eat and have some left over.'"*

**Elisha tells Naaman How to be Healed of Leprosy**
   *– 2 Kings 5:1-19*
*¹⁰ Elisha sent a messenger to say to him, "Go, wash yourself
seven times in the Jordan, and your flesh will be restored and
you will be cleansed."*
*¹⁴ So he went down and dipped himself in the Jordan seven
times, as the man of God had told him, and his flesh was
restored and became clean like that of a young boy.*

**The Blinded Syrians Captured** – 2 Kings 6:8-23
*¹⁸ As the enemy came down toward him, Elisha prayed to
the LORD, "Strike this army with blindness." So he struck them
with blindness, as Elisha had asked.*

## ESTHER

**Esther Becomes Queen** – Esther 2:1-18
*¹⁷ Now the king was attracted to Esther more than to any of the
other women, and she won his favor and approval more than any
of the other virgins. So he set a royal crown on her head and
made her queen instead of Vashti.*

**A Plot against the Jews** – Esther 2:19 - 3:15

*21 During the time Mordecai was sitting at the king's gate, Bigthana and Teresh, two of the king's officers who guarded the doorway, became angry and conspired to assassinate King Xerxes. 22 But Mordecai found out about the plot and told Queen Esther, who in turn reported it to the king, giving credit to Mordecai.*

**For Such a Time as This** – Esther 4:1-17

*12 When Esther's words were reported to Mordecai, 13 he sent back this answer: "Do not think that because you are in the king's house you alone of all the Jews will escape. 14 For if you remain silent at this time, relief and deliverance for the Jews will arise from another place, but you and your father's family will perish. And who knows but that you have come to your royal position for such a time as this?"*

**Esther's Banquet** – Esther 5:1-8

*3 Then the king asked, "What is it, Queen Esther? What is your request? Even up to half the kingdom, it will be given you."4 "If it pleases the king," replied Esther, "let the king, together with Haman, come today to a banquet I have prepared for him."*

**Haman Hanged Instead of Mordecai** – Esther 7:1-10

*9 Then Harbona, one of the eunuchs attending the king, said, "A pole reaching to a height of fifty cubits[a] stands by Haman's house. He had it set up for Mordecai, who spoke up to help the king." The king said, "Impale him on it!" 10 So they impaled Haman on the pole he had set up for Mordecai.*

## EZEKIEL

**Ezekiel's Vision of God** – Ezekiel 1:1-28

*26 Above the vault over their heads was what looked like a throne of lapis lazuli, and high above on the throne was a figure like that of a man. 27 I saw that from what appeared to be his waist up he looked like glowing metal, as if full of fire, and that from there down he looked like fire; and brilliant light surrounded him. 28 Like the appearance of a rainbow in the*

*clouds on a rainy day, so was the radiance around him. This was
the appearance of the likeness of the glory of the LORD. When I
saw it, I fell facedown, and I heard the voice of one speaking.*

### The Watchman & His Message – Ezekiel 33:1-11
*⁷ "Son of man, I have made you a watchman for the people of
Israel; so hear the word I speak and give them warning from
me."*

### Dry Bones Live – Ezekiel 37:1-14
*⁴ Then he said to me, "Prophesy to these bones and say to them,
'Dry bones, hear the word of the LORD! ⁵ This is what the
Sovereign LORD says to these bones: I will make breath enter
you, and you will come to life. ⁶ I will attach tendons to you and
make flesh come upon you and cover you with skin; I will put
breath in you, and you will come to life. Then you will know that
I am the LORD.'"*

## <u>GIDEON</u>

### Gideon: Mighty Man of Valor – Judges 6:11-27
*¹² When the angel of the LORD appeared to Gideon, he said,
"The LORD is with you, mighty warrior."*

### Gideon Destroys the Temple of Baal – Judges 6:28-35
*²⁸ In the morning when the people of the town got up, there was
Baal's altar, demolished, with the Asherah pole beside it cut
down and the second bull sacrificed on the newly built altar!
²⁹ They asked each other, "Who did this?" When they carefully
investigated, they were told, "Gideon son of Joash did it."*

### The Sign of the Fleece – Judges 6:36-40
*³⁶ Gideon said to God, "If you will save Israel by my hand as you
have promised— ³⁷ look, I will place a wool fleece on the
threshing floor. If there is dew only on the fleece and all the
ground is dry, then I will know that you will save Israel by my
hand, as you said." ³⁸ And that is what happened. Gideon rose
early the next day; he squeezed the fleece and wrung out the
dew—a bowlful of water.*

**Gideon's Army of 300 Soldiers** – Judges 7:1-25
*² The LORD said to Gideon, "You have too many men. I cannot deliver Midian into their hands, or Israel would boast against me, 'My own strength has saved me.'*
*⁸ So Gideon sent the rest of the Israelites home but kept the three hundred, who took over the provisions and trumpets of the others.*

## ISAAC

**Isaac Is Born** – Genesis 21:1-7
*¹ Now the LORD was gracious to Sarah as he had said, and the LORD did for Sarah what he had promised. ² Sarah became pregnant and bore a son to Abraham in his old age, at the very time God had promised him. ³ Abraham gave the name Isaac to the son Sarah bore him.*

**A Bride for Isaac** – Genesis 24:1-67
*¹² Then he prayed, "LORD, God of my master Abraham, make me successful today, and show kindness to my master Abraham. ¹³ See, I am standing beside this spring, and the daughters of the townspeople are coming out to draw water. ¹⁴ May it be that when I say to a young woman, 'Please let down your jar that I may have a drink,' and she says, 'Drink, and I'll water your camels too'—let her be the one you have chosen for your servant Isaac. By this I will know that you have shown kindness to my master."*
*¹⁵ Before he had finished praying, Rebekah came out with her jar on her shoulder.*

**Isaac and Abimelek** – Genesis 26:1-35
*¹¹ So Abimelek gave orders to all the people: "Anyone who harms this man or his wife shall surely be put to death."*

**Isaac Blesses Jacob** – Genesis 27:1-29
*²⁸ May God give you heaven's dew and earth's richness—an abundance of grain and new wine. ²⁹ May nations serve you and peoples bow down to you. Be lord over your brothers, and may*

*the sons of your mother bow down to you. May those who curse you be cursed and those who bless you be blessed."*

**Death of Isaac** – Genesis 35:27-29
*²⁸ Isaac lived a hundred and eighty years. ²⁹ Then he breathed his last and died and was gathered to his people, old and full of years. And his sons Esau and Jacob buried him.*

## JACOB

**Jacob and Esau are Born** – Genesis 25:12-28
*²³ The LORD said to her, "Two nations are in your womb, and two peoples from within you will be separated; one people will be stronger than the other, and the older will serve the younger."²⁴ When the time came for her to give birth, there were twin boys in her womb. ²⁵ The first to come out was red, and his whole body was like a hairy garment; so they named him Esau. ²⁶ After this, his brother came out, with his hand grasping Esau's heel; so he was named Jacob Isaac was sixty years old when Rebekah gave birth to them.*

**Isaac Blesses Jacob** – Genesis 27:1-29
*²⁸ May God give you heaven's dew and earth's richness—an abundance of grain and new wine.*
*²⁹ May nations serve you and peoples bow down to you. Be lord over your brothers, and may the sons of your mother bow down to you. May those who curse you be cursed and those who bless you be blessed."*

**Jacob's Ladder** – Genesis 28:10-22
*¹² He had a dream in which he saw a stairway resting on the earth, with its top reaching to heaven, and the angels of God were ascending and descending on it. ¹³ There above it stood the LORD, and he said: "I am the LORD, the God of your father Abraham and the God of Isaac. I will give you and your descendants the land on which you are lying. ¹⁴ Your descendants will be like the dust of the earth, and you will spread out to the west and to the east, to the north and to the south. All peoples on earth will be blessed through you and your offspring. ¹⁵ I am with*

*you and will watch over you wherever you go, and I will bring
you back to this land. I will not leave you until I have done what
I have promised you."*

**Jacob Meets Rachel** – Genesis 29:1-14
*10 When Jacob saw Rachel daughter of his uncle Laban, and
Laban's sheep, he went over and rolled the stone away from the
mouth of the well and watered his uncle's sheep. 11 Then Jacob
kissed Rachel and began to weep aloud. 12 He had told Rachel
that he was a relative of her father and a son of Rebekah. So she
ran and told her father.*

**Jacob Marries Leah & Rachel** – Genesis 29:15-30
*16 Now Laban had two daughters; the name of the older was
Leah, and the name of the younger was Rachel. 17 Leah had
weak eyes, but Rachel had a lovely figure and was beautiful.*

**Jacob's Agreement with Laban** – Genesis 30:25-43
*31 "What shall I give you?" he asked. "Don't give me anything,"
Jacob replied. "But if you will do this one thing for me, I will go
on tending your flocks and watching over them: 32 Let me go
through all your flocks today and remove from them every
speckled or spotted sheep, every dark-colored lamb and every
spotted or speckled goat. They will be my wages.*

**Jacob Flees from Laban** – Genesis 31:1-55
*1 Jacob heard that Laban's sons were saying, "Jacob has taken
everything our father owned and has gained all this wealth from
what belonged to our father." 2 And Jacob noticed that Laban's
attitude toward him was not what it had been. 3 Then
the LORD said to Jacob, "Go back to the land of your fathers and
to your relatives, and I will be with you."*

**Jacob Wrestles with God** – Genesis 32:22-32
*24 So Jacob was left alone, and a man wrestled with him till
daybreak. 25 When the man saw that he could not overpower him,
he touched the socket of Jacob's hip so that his hip was
wrenched as he wrestled with the man.*

**Jacob's Journey to Egypt** – Genesis 46:1 - 47:12
*² And God spoke to Israel in a vision at night and said, "Jacob! Jacob!" "Here I am," he replied.*
*³ "I am God, the God of your father," he said. "Do not be afraid to go down to Egypt, for I will make you into a great nation there. ⁴ I will go down to Egypt with you, and I will surely bring you back again. And Joseph's own hand will close your eyes."*

**Jacob Blesses Joseph's Sons** – Genesis 48:1-22
*¹⁴ But Israel reached out his right hand and put it on Ephraim's head, though he was the younger, and crossing his arms, he put his left hand on Manasseh's head, even though Manasseh was the firstborn.*

**Jacob's Last Words to His Sons** – Genesis 49:1-28
*²⁸ All these are the twelve tribes of Israel, and this is what their father said to them when he blessed them, giving each the blessing appropriate to him.*

## <u>JESUS</u>

The teachings of Jesus can be found throughout the New Testament. His Birth, Life, Death and Resurrection are recorded in the gospels of Matthew, Mark, Luke and John.
John 21:25 *Jesus did many other things as well. If every one of them were written down, I suppose that even the whole world would not have room for the books that would be written.*

## <u>JONAH</u>

**Jonah's Disobedience** – Jonah 1:1-3
*³ But Jonah ran away from the LORD and headed for Tarshish. He went down to Joppa, where he found a ship bound for that port. After paying the fare, he went aboard and sailed for Tarshish to flee from the LORD.*

**The Storm at Sea** – Jonah 1:4-9
*⁴ Then the LORD sent a great wind on the sea, and such a violent storm arose that the ship threatened to break up.*

**Jonah Thrown into the Sea** – Jonah 1:10-16
*¹² "Pick me up and throw me into the sea," he replied, "and it will become calm. I know that it is my fault that this great storm has come upon you."*

**Jonah's Prayer and Deliverance** – Jonah 1:17 - 2:10
*¹ From inside the fish Jonah prayed to the Lord his God. 2 He said: "In my distress I called to the Lord, and he answered me. From deep in the realm of the dead I called for help, and you listened to my cry.*

**Jonah Preaches at Nineveh** – Jonah 3:1-4
*³ Jonah obeyed the word of the LORD and went to Nineveh.*

**The People of Nineveh Believe** – Jonah 3:5-10
*⁵ The Ninevites believed God. A fast was proclaimed, and all of them, from the greatest to the least, put on sackcloth.*

## <u>JOSEPH</u>

**Joseph Dreams of Greatness** – Genesis 37:1-11
*⁵ Joseph had a dream, and when he told it to his brothers, they hated him all the more.*

**Joseph Sold by His Brothers** – Genesis 37:12-36
*²⁶ Judah said to his brothers, "What will we gain if we kill our brother and cover up his blood? ²⁷ Come, let's sell him to the Ishmaelites and not lay our hands on him; after all, he is our brother, our own flesh and blood." His brothers agreed. ²⁸ So when the Midianite merchants came by, his brothers pulled Joseph up out of the cistern and sold him for twenty shekels of silver to the Ishmaelites, who took him to Egypt.*

**Joseph a Slave in Egypt** – Genesis 39:1-23

*²The LORD was with Joseph so that he prospered, and he lived in the house of his Egyptian master. ³When his master saw that the LORD was with him and that the LORD gave him success in everything he did,⁴Joseph found favor in his eyes and became his attendant. Potiphar put him in charge of his household, and he entrusted to his care everything he owned.*

**Joseph Interprets the Prisoners' Dreams** – Genesis 40:1-23

*²The LORD was with Joseph so that he prospered, and he lived in the house of his Egyptian master. ³When his master saw that the LORD was with him and that the LORD gave him success in everything he did,⁴Joseph found favor in his eyes and became his attendant. Potiphar put him in charge of his household, and he entrusted to his care everything he owned.*

**Joseph Interprets Pharaoh's Dreams** – Genesis 41:1-36

*¹⁵Pharaoh said to Joseph, "I had a dream, and no one can interpret it. But I have heard it said of you that when you hear a dream you can interpret it." ¹⁶"I cannot do it," Joseph replied to Pharaoh, "but God will give Pharaoh the answer he desires."*

**Joseph's Rise to Power** – Genesis 41:37-57

*³⁹Then Pharaoh said to Joseph, "Since God has made all this known to you, there is no one so discerning and wise as you. ⁴⁰You shall be in charge of my palace, and all my people are to submit to your orders. Only with respect to the throne will I be greater than you."*

**Joseph's Brothers Go to Egypt** – Genesis 42:1-38

*³Then ten of Joseph's brothers went down to buy grain from Egypt. ⁴But Jacob did not send Benjamin, Joseph's brother, with the others, because he was afraid that harm might come to him. ⁵So Israel's sons were among those who went to buy grain, for there was famine in the land of Canaan also.*

**Joseph Meets Benjamin** – Genesis 43:1-34

*²⁹As he looked about and saw his brother Benjamin, his own mother's son, he asked, "Is this your youngest brother, the one you told me about?" And he said, "God be gracious to you, my son." [30] Deeply moved at the sight of his brother, Joseph hurried out and looked for a place to weep. He went into his private room and wept there.*

**Joseph's Cup** – Genesis 44:1-17
*[1] Now Joseph gave these instructions to the steward of his house: "Fill the men's sacks with as much food as they can carry, and put each man's silver in the mouth of his sack. [2] Then put my cup, the silver one, in the mouth of the youngest one's sack, along with the silver for his grain." And he did as Joseph said.*

**Joseph Revealed to His Brothers** – Genesis 45:1-28
*[3] Joseph said to his brothers, "I am Joseph! Is my father still living?" But his brothers were not able to answer him, because they were terrified at his presence.*

**Joseph Deals with the Famine** – Genesis 47:13-26
*[20] So Joseph bought all the land in Egypt for Pharaoh. The Egyptians, one and all, sold their fields, because the famine was too severe for them. The land became Pharaoh's, [21] and Joseph reduced the people to servitude, from one end of Egypt to the other.*

**Joseph's Vow to Jacob** – Genesis 47:27-31
*[29] When the time drew near for Israel to die, he called for his son Joseph and said to him, "If I have found favor in your eyes, put your hand under my thigh and promise that you will show me kindness and faithfulness. Do not bury me in Egypt, [30] but when I rest with my fathers, carry me out of Egypt and bury me where they are buried." "I will do as you say," he said.*

**Jacob Blesses Joseph's Sons** – Genesis 48:1-22
*[15] Then he blessed Joseph and said, "May the God before whom my fathers Abraham and Isaac walked faithfully, the God who has been my shepherd all my life to this day, [16] the Angel who has delivered me from all harm —may he bless these boys. May they*

*be called by my name and the names of my fathers Abraham and Isaac, and may they increase greatly on the earth."*

**Death of Joseph** – Genesis 50:22-26
*²⁶ So Joseph died at the age of a hundred and ten. And after they embalmed him, he was placed in a coffin in Egypt.*

## JOSHUA

**Joshua to Succeed Moses** – Numbers 27:12-23
*¹⁸ So the LORD said to Moses, "Take Joshua son of Nun, a man in whom is the spirit of leadership, and lay your hand on him. ¹⁹ Have him stand before Eleazar the priest and the entire assembly and commission him in their presence. ²⁰ Give him some of your authority so the whole Israelite community will obey him.*

**God's Commission to Joshua** – Joshua 1:1-9
*After the death of Moses the servant of the LORD, the LORD said to Joshua son of Nun, Moses' aide: ² "Moses my servant is dead. Now then, you and all these people, get ready to cross the Jordan River into the land I am about to give to them—to the Israelites. ³ I will give you every place where you set your foot, as I promised Moses. ⁹ Have I not commanded you? Be strong and courageous. Do not be afraid; do not be discouraged, for the LORD your God will be with you wherever you go."*

**Rahab Hides the Spies** – Joshua 2:1-24
*⁸ Before the spies lay down for the night, she went up on the roof ⁹ and said to them, "I know that the LORD has given you this land and that a great fear of you has fallen on us, so that all who live in this country are melting in fear because of you. ⁸ Before the spies lay down for the night, she went up on the roof ⁹ and said to them, "I know that the LORD has given you this land and that a great fear of you has fallen on us, so that all who live in this country are melting in fear because of you.*

**Israel Crosses the Jordan** – Joshua 3:1-17
*¹⁷ The priests who carried the ark of the covenant of the LORD stopped in the middle of the Jordan and stood on dry ground, while*

*all Israel passed by until the whole nation had completed the crossing on dry ground.*

### Walls of Jericho – Joshua 6:1-27

*[20] When the trumpets sounded, the army shouted, and at the sound of the trumpet, when the men gave a loud shout, the wall collapsed; so everyone charged straight in, and they took the city.*

### The Sun Stands Still – Joshua 10:1-15

*[13] So the sun stood still, and the moon stopped, till the nation avenged itself on its enemies, as it is written in the Book of Jashar. The sun stopped in the middle of the sky and delayed going down about a full day.*

## MOSES

### Moses is Born – Exodus 2:1-10

*[1] Now a man of the tribe of Levi married a Levite woman, [2] and she became pregnant and gave birth to a son. When she saw that he was a fine child, she hid him for three months. [3] But when she could hide him no longer, she got a papyrus basket for him and coated it with tar and pitch. Then she placed the child in it and put it among the reeds along the bank of the Nile.*

### The Burning Bush – Exodus 3:1-22

*[1] Now Moses was tending the flock of Jethro his father-in-law, the priest of Midian, and he led the flock to the far side of the wilderness and came to Horeb, the mountain of God. [2] There the angel of the LORD appeared to him in flames of fire from within a bush. Moses saw that though the bush was on fire it did not burn up.*

### Plagues on Egypt – Exodus 7:14 - 12:30

*[1] Then the LORD said to Moses, "See, I have made you like God to Pharaoh, and your brother Aaron will be your prophet. [2] You are to say everything I command you, and your brother Aaron is to tell Pharaoh to let the Israelites go out of his country. [3] But I will harden Pharaoh's heart, and though I multiply my signs and wonders in Egypt, [4] he will not listen to*

*you. Then I will lay my hand on Egypt and with mighty acts of judgment I will bring out my divisions, my people the Israelites. ⁵ And the Egyptians will know that I am the LORD when I stretch out my hand against Egypt and bring the Israelites out of it."*

**The Exodus** – Exodus 12:31-42
*³¹ During the night Pharaoh summoned Moses and Aaron and said, "Up! Leave my people, you and the Israelites! Go, worship the LORD as you have requested. ³² Take your flocks and herds, as you have said, and go. And also bless me."*

**Red Sea Crossing** – Exodus 14:1-19
*¹³ Moses answered the people, "Do not be afraid. Stand firm and you will see the deliverance the LORD will bring you today. The Egyptians you see today you will never see again. ¹⁴ The LORD will fight for you; you need only to be still."¹⁵ Then the LORD said to Moses, "Why are you crying out to me? Tell the Israelites to move on. ¹⁶ Raise your staff and stretch out your hand over the sea to divide the water so that the Israelites can go through the sea on dry ground.*

**Manna from Heaven** – Exodus 16:1-36
*⁴ Then the LORD said to Moses, "I will rain down bread from heaven for you. The people are to go out each day and gather enough for that day. In this way I will test them and see whether they will follow my instructions.*

**Water from the Rock** – Exodus 17:1-7
*⁵ The LORD answered Moses, "Go out in front of the people. Take with you some of the elders of Israel and take in your hand the staff with which you struck the Nile, and go. ⁶ I will stand there before you by the rock at Horeb. Strike the rock, and water will come out of it for the people to drink." So Moses did this in the sight of the elders of Israel.*

**The Ten Commandments** – Exodus 20:1-17
*[1]And God spoke all these words:[2] "I am the LORD your God, who brought you out of Egypt, out of the land of slavery.[3] "You shall have no other gods before me.*

**The Greatest Commandment** – Deuteronomy 6:1-9
*[5]Love the LORD your God with all your heart and with all your soul and with all your strength.*

**The Cloud & the Fire** – Numbers 9:15-23
*[15]On the day the tabernacle, the tent of the covenant law, was set up, the cloud covered it. From evening till morning the cloud above the tabernacle looked like fire. [16]That is how it continued to be; the cloud covered it, and at night it looked like fire.*

**The Lord sends Quail** – Numbers 11:31-35
*[31]Now a wind went out from the LORD and drove quail in from the sea. It scattered them up to two cubits deep all around the camp, as far as a day's walk in any direction. [32]All that day and night and all the next day the people went out and gathered quail. No one gathered less than ten homers.[b] Then they spread them out all around the camp.*

**Spies sent to Canaan** – Numbers 13:1-33
*[27]They gave Moses this account: "We went into the land to which you sent us, and it does flow with milk and honey! Here is its fruit. [28]But the people who live there are powerful, and the cities are fortified and very large. We even saw descendants of Anak there.*

**Aaron's Rod Buds** – Numbers 17:1-13
*[8]The next day Moses entered the tent and saw that Aaron's staff, which represented the tribe of Levi, had not only sprouted but had budded, blossomed and produced almonds.*

**The Bronze Serpent** – Numbers 21:4-9
*[8]The LORD said to Moses, "Make a snake and put it up on a pole; anyone who is bitten can look at it and live." [9]So Moses*

*made a bronze snake and put it up on a pole. Then when anyone was bitten by a snake and looked at the bronze snake, they lived.*

**The Desert Years** – Deuteronomy 2:1-25
*⁷ The LORD your God has blessed you in all the work of your hands. He has watched over your journey through this vast wilderness. These forty years the LORD your God has been with you, and you have not lacked anything.*

**Moses Denied Entrance to the Promised Land**
     – Deuteronomy 3:23-29
*²⁷ Go up to the top of Pisgah and look west and north and south and east. Look at the land with your own eyes, since you are not going to cross this Jordan. ²⁸ But commission Joshua, and encourage and strengthen him, for he will lead this people across and will cause them to inherit the land that you will see.*

**Joshua New Leader of Israel** – Deuteronomy 31:1-8
*⁷ Then Moses summoned Joshua and said to him in the presence of all Israel, "Be strong and courageous, for you must go with this people into the land that the LORD swore to their ancestors to give them, and you must divide it among them as their inheritance. ⁸ The LORD himself goes before you and will be with you; he will never leave you nor forsake you. Do not be afraid; do not be discouraged."*

**Moses Dies on Mount Nebo** – Deuteronomy 32:48 - 34:12
*⁴⁸ On that same day the LORD told Moses, ⁴⁹ "Go up into the Abarim Range to Mount Nebo in Moab, across from Jericho, and view Canaan, the land I am giving the Israelites as their own possession. ⁵⁰ There on the mountain that you have climbed you will die and be gathered to your people, just as your brother Aaron died on Mount Hor and was gathered to his people.*

## NAAMAN

**Naaman's Leprosy Healed** – 2 Kings 5:1-19
*¹⁰ Elisha sent a messenger to say to him, "Go, wash yourself seven times in the Jordan, and your flesh will be restored and you will be cleansed."*
*¹⁴ So he went down and dipped himself in the Jordan seven times, as the man of God had told him, and his flesh was restored and became clean like that of a young boy.*

## NOAH

**Noah Pleases God** – Genesis 6:1-12
*⁹ Noah was a righteous man, blameless among the people of his time, and he walked faithfully with God.*

**God's Command to Noah** – Genesis 6:13-14
*¹³ So God said to Noah, "I am going to put an end to all people, for the earth is filled with violence because of them. I am surely going to destroy both them and the earth. ¹⁴ So make yourself an ark of cypress wood; make rooms in it and coat it with pitch inside and out.*

**Noah Prepares the Ark** – Genesis 6:13-22
*²² Noah did everything just as God commanded him.*

**The Great Flood** – Genesis 7:1-24
*¹¹ In the six hundredth year of Noah's life, on the seventeenth day of the second month—on that day all the springs of the great deep burst forth, and the floodgates of the heavens were opened. ¹² And rain fell on the earth forty days and forty nights.*

**Noah's Deliverance** – Genesis 8:1-19
¹ But God remembered Noah and all the wild animals and the livestock that were with him in the ark, and he sent a wind over the earth, and the waters receded.

**God's Covenant with Creation** – Genesis 8:20-22

*21 "Never again will I curse the ground because of humans, even though every inclination of the human heart is evil from childhood. And never again will I destroy all living creatures, as I have done. 22 "As long as the earth endures, seedtime and harvest, cold and heat, summer and winter, day and night will never cease."*

**God's Promise to Noah** – Genesis 9:1-17

*12 And God said, "This is the sign of the covenant I am making between me and you and every living creature with you, a covenant for all generations to come: 13 I have set my rainbow in the clouds, and it will be the sign of the covenant between me and the earth.*

## RUTH

**Naomi Returns with Ruth** – Ruth 1:1-22

*12 Return home, my daughters; I am too old to have another husband. Even if I thought there was still hope for me—even if I had a husband tonight and then gave birth to sons*
*16 But Ruth replied, "Don't urge me to leave you or to turn back from you. Where you go I will go, and where you stay I will stay. Your people will be my people and your God my God. 17 Where you die I will die, and there I will be buried. May the LORD deal with me, be it ever so severely, if even death separates you and me."*

**Ruth Meets Boaz** – Ruth 2:1-23

*8 So Boaz said to Ruth, "My daughter, listen to me. Don't go and glean in another field and don't go away from here. Stay here with the women who work for me.*

**Boaz Redeems Ruth** – Ruth 4:1-12

*9 Then Boaz announced to the elders and all the people, "Today you are witnesses that I have bought from Naomi all the property of Elimelek, Kilion and Mahlon. 10 I have also acquired Ruth the Moabite, Mahlon's widow, as my wife, in order to maintain the name of the dead with his property, so that his name will not disappear from among his family or from his hometown. Today you are witnesses!"*

## <u>SAMSON</u>

**The Birth of Samson** – Judges 13:1-25
*[24] The woman gave birth to a boy and named him Samson. He grew and the LORD blessed him, [25] and the Spirit of the LORD began to stir him while he was in Mahaneh Dan, between Zorah and Eshtaol.*

**Samson's Philistine Wife** – Judges 14:1-20
*[1] Samson went down to Timnah and saw there a young Philistine woman. [2] When he returned, he said to his father and mother, "I have seen a Philistine woman in Timnah; now get her for me as my wife."*

**Samson Defeats the Philistines** – Judges 15:1-20
*[15] Finding a fresh jawbone of a donkey, he grabbed it and struck down a thousand men.*

**Samson & Delilah** – Judges 16:1-22
*[4] Some time later, he fell in love with a woman in the Valley of Sorek whose name was Delilah. [5] The rulers of the Philistines went to her and said, "See if you can lure him into showing you the secret of his great strength and how we can overpower him so we may tie him up and subdue him. Each one of us will give you eleven hundred shekels of silver."*

**Samson Dies with the Philistines** – Judges 16:23-31
*[28] Then Samson prayed to the LORD, "Sovereign LORD, remember me. Please, God, strengthen me just once more, and let me with one blow get revenge on the Philistines for my two eyes." [29] Then Samson reached toward the two central pillars on which the temple stood. Bracing himself against them, his right hand on the one and his left hand on the other, [30] Samson said, "Let me die with the Philistines!" Then he pushed with all his might, and down came the temple on the rulers and all the people in it. Thus he killed many more when he died than while he lived.*

## SAMUEL

**Hannah's Vow** – 1 Samuel 1:8-18
*11 And she made a vow, saying, "LORD Almighty, if you will only look on your servant's misery and remember me, and not forget your servant but give her a son, then I will give him to the LORD for all the days of his life, and no razor will ever be used on his head."*

**Samuel is Born** – 1 Samuel 1:19-28
*20 So in the course of time Hannah became pregnant and gave birth to a son. She named him Samuel, saying, "Because I asked the LORD for him."*
**God Calls Samuel** – 1 Samuel 3:1-10
*10 The LORD came and stood there, calling as at the other times, "Samuel! Samuel!"*
*Then Samuel said, "Speak, for your servant is listening."*

**Samuel's Childhood Ministry** – 1 Samuel 2:18-21
*18 But Samuel was ministering before the LORD—a boy wearing a linen ephod.*

**Samuel's First Prophecy** – 1 Samuel 3:11-21
*15 Samuel lay down until morning and then opened the doors of the house of the LORD. He was afraid to tell Eli the vision, 16 but Eli called him and said, "Samuel, my son." Samuel answered, "Here I am." 17 "What was it he said to you?" Eli asked. "Do not hide it from me. May God deal with you, be it ever so severely, if you hide from me anything he told you."*

## SAUL

**Israel Demands a King** – 1 Samuel 8:1-22
*4 So all the elders of Israel gathered together and came to Samuel at Ramah. 5 They said to him, "You are old, and your sons do not follow your ways; now appoint a king to lead us, such as all the other nations have."*

**Saul Chosen as King** – 1 Samuel 9:1 - 10:27

*10:1 Then Samuel took a flask of olive oil and poured it on Saul's head and kissed him, saying, "Has not the LORD anointed you ruler over his inheritance?*

**Jonathan Defeats the Philistines** – 1 Samuel 14:1-23

*6 Jonathan said to his young armor-bearer, "Come, let's go over to the outpost of those uncircumcised men. Perhaps the LORD will act in our behalf. Nothing can hinder the LORD from saving, whether by many or by few."*

**Saul Rejected as King** – 1 Samuel 15:10-35

*10 Then the word of the LORD came to Samuel: 11 "I regret that I have made Saul king, because he has turned away from me and has not carried out my instructions."*

**Saul Resents David** – 1 Samuel 18:1-16

*6 When the men were returning home after David had killed the Philistine, the women came out from all the towns of Israel to meet King Saul with singing and dancing, with joyful songs and with timbrels and lyres. 7 As they danced, they sang: "Saul has slain his thousands, and David his tens of thousands."*
*8 Saul was very angry; this refrain displeased him greatly. "They have credited David with tens of thousands," he thought, "but me with only thousands. What more can he get but the kingdom?" 9 And from that time on Saul kept a close eye on David.*

**Death of Saul & His Sons** – 1 Samuel 31:1-13

*6 So Saul and his three sons and his armor-bearer and all his men died together that same day.*

## SOLOMON

**The Birth of Solomon** – 2 Samuel 12:24-25

*24 Then David comforted his wife Bathsheba, and he went to her and made love to her. She gave birth to a son, and they named him Solomon. The LORD loved him*

**Bathsheba Defends Solomon's Right as King** – 1 Kings 1:11-27
*[17] She said to him, "My lord, you yourself swore to me your servant by the LORD your God: 'Solomon your son shall be king after me, and he will sit on my throne.'*

**David Proclaims Solomon King** – 1 Kings 1:28-53
*[29] The king then took an oath: "As surely as the LORD lives, who has delivered me out of every trouble, [30] I will surely carry out this very day what I swore to you by the LORD, the God of Israel: Solomon your son shall be king after me, and he will sit on my throne in my place."*

**David's Instructions to Solomon** – 1 Kings 2:1-9
*[2] "I am about to go the way of all the earth," he said. "So be strong, act like a man, [3] and observe what the LORD your God requires: Walk in obedience to him, and keep his decrees and commands, his laws and regulations, as written in the Law of Moses. Do this so that you may prosper in all you do and wherever you go*

**Solomon Requests Faith** – 1 Kings 3:1-15
*[7] "Now, LORD my God, you have made your servant king in place of my father David. But I am only a little child and do not know how to carry out my duties. [8] Your servant is here among the people you have chosen, a great people, too numerous to count or number. [9] So give your servant a discerning heart to govern your people and to distinguish between right and wrong. For who is able to govern this great people of yours?"*

**Solomon's Wise Judgement** – 1 Kings 3:16-28
*[23] The king said, "This one says, 'My son is alive and your son is dead,' while that one says, 'No! Your son is dead and mine is alive.'" [24] Then the king said, "Bring me a sword." So they brought a sword for the king. [25] He then gave an order: "Cut the living child in two and give half to one and half to the other."*

**Solomon's Wisdom** – 1 Kings 4:29-34
*[29] God gave Solomon wisdom and very great insight, and a breadth of understanding as measureless as the sand on the seashore. [30] Solomon's wisdom was greater than the wisdom of all the people of the East, and greater than all the wisdom of Egypt.*

**Solomon Builds the Temple** – 1 Kings 5:1 - 6:38
*13 King Solomon conscripted laborers from all Israel—thirty thousand men.*

**God's Second Appearance to Solomon** – 1 Kings 9:1-9
*1 When Solomon had finished building the temple of the LORD and the royal palace, and had achieved all he had desired to do, 2 the LORD appeared to him a second time, as he had appeared to him at Gibeon.*

**Queen of Sheba Praises Solomon** – 1 Kings 10:1-13
*6 She said to the king, "The report I heard in my own country about your achievements and your wisdom is true. 7 But I did not believe these things until I came and saw with my own eyes. Indeed, not even half was told me; in wisdom and wealth you have far exceeded the report I heard. 8 How happy your people must be! How happy your officials, who continually stand before you and hear your wisdom! 9 Praise be to the LORD your God, who has delighted in you and placed you on the throne of Israel. Because of the LORD's eternal love for Israel, he has made you king to maintain justice and righteousness."*

**Solomon's Great Wealth** – 1 Kings 10:14-29
*14 The weight of the gold that Solomon received yearly was 666 talents, 15 not including the revenues from merchants and traders and from all the Arabian kings and the governors of the territories.*

**Solomon Turns from the Lord** – 1 Kings 11:1-13
*9 The LORD became angry with Solomon because his heart had turned away from the LORD, the God of Israel, who had appeared to him twice. 10 Although he had forbidden Solomon to follow other gods, Solomon did not keep the LORD's command. 11 So the LORD said to Solomon, "Since this is your attitude and you have not kept my covenant and my decrees, which I commanded you, I will most certainly tear the kingdom away from you and give it to one of your subordinates.*

# <u>PRAYERS</u>

**Hannah's Prayer** – 1 Samuel 2:1-11
*¹ My heart rejoices in the LORD; in the LORD my horn is lifted high. My mouth boasts over my enemies, for I delight in your deliverance.*

**Solomon's Prayer of Dedication** – 1 Kings 8:22-53
*²³ LORD, the God of Israel, there is no God like you in heaven above or on earth below—you who keep your covenant of love with your servants who continue wholeheartedly in your way...*

**Hezekiah's Prayer against Sennacherib's Threat**
    - Isaiah 37:8-20
*¹⁶ LORD Almighty, the God of Israel, enthroned between the cherubim, you alone are God over all the kingdoms of the earth. You have made heaven and earth. ¹⁷ Give ear, LORD, and hear; open your eyes, LORD, and see; listen to all the words Sennacherib has sent to ridicule the living God.*

**David's Prayer** – 1 Chronicles 17:16-27
*¹⁶ Then King David went in and sat before the LORD, and he said: "Who am I, LORD God, and what is my family, that you have brought me this far?*
1 Chronicles
*¹⁴ "But who am I, and who are my people, that we should be able to give as generously as this? Everything comes from you, and we have given you only what comes from your hand.*

**Solomon's Prayer of Dedication** – 2 Chronicles 6:12-42
*¹⁵ LORD, the God of Israel, there is no God like you in heaven or on earth—you who keep your covenant of love with your servants who continue wholeheartedly in your way.*

**Fasting and Prayer for Protection** – Ezra 8:21-23
*²³ So we fasted and petitioned our God about this, and he answered our prayer.*

**Nehemiah Prays for His People** – Nehemiah 1:1-11
*5 LORD, the God of heaven, the great and awesome God, who keeps his covenant of love with those who love him and keep his commandments, 6 let your ear be attentive and your eyes open to hear the prayer your servant is praying before you day and night for your servants, the people of Israel...*

**Job's Despondent Prayer** – Job 13:20 – 14:22
*23 How many wrongs and sins have I committed? Show me my offense and my sin. 24 Why do you hide your face and consider me your enemy?*

**A Prayer for Guidance** – Psalm 5:1-12
*1 Listen to my words, LORD, consider my lament. 2 Hear my cry for help, my King and my God, for to you I pray. 3 In the morning, LORD, you hear my voice; in the morning I lay my requests before you and wait expectantly.*

**A Prayer for Faith in Time of Distress** – Psalm 6:1-10
*2 Have mercy on me, LORD, for I am faint; heal me, LORD, for my bones are in agony.*

**Prayer and Praise for Deliverance from Enemies**
    – Psalm 7:1-17
*1 LORD my God, I take refuge in you; save and deliver me from all who pursue me, 2 or they will tear me apart like a lion and rip me to pieces with no one to rescue me.*

**Prayer and Thanksgiving for the Lord's Righteous**
    **Judgements** – Psalm 9:1-20
*3 My enemies turn back; they stumble and perish before you. 4 For you have upheld my right and my cause, sitting enthroned as the righteous judge.*

**Prayer with Confidence in Final Salvation** – Psalm 17:1-15
*1 Hear me, LORD, my plea is just; listen to my cry. Hear my prayer— it does not rise from deceitful lips. 2 Let my vindication come from you; may your eyes see what is right.*

**A Prayer for Divine Scrutiny and Redemption**
    – Psalm 26:1-12
*² Test me, LORD, and try me, examine my heart and my mind;*
*³ for I have always been mindful of your unfailing love and have
lived in reliance on your faithfulness.*

**A Prayer for Mercy** – Psalm 28:1-9
*² Hear my cry for mercy as I call to you for help, as I lift up my
hands toward your Most Holy Place.*

**The Blessedness of Answered Prayer** – Psalm 30:1-12
*¹¹ You turned my wailing into dancing; you removed my
sackcloth and clothed me with joy, ¹² that my heart may sing your
praises and not be silent. LORD my God, I will praise you
forever.*

**Prayer in Time of Chastening** – Psalm 38:1-22
*²¹ LORD, do not forsake me; do not be far from me, my God.*
*²² Come quickly to help me, my Lord and my Savior.*

**Prayer for Wisdom and Forgiveness** – Psalm 39:1-13
*⁸ Save me from all my transgressions; do not make me the
scorn of fools.*

**Prayer to God in Time of Trouble** – Psalm 43:1-5
*³ Send me your light and your faithful care, let them lead me;
let them bring me to your holy mountain, to the place where you
dwell.*

**A Prayer of Repentance** – Psalm 51:1-19
*¹ Have mercy on me, O God, according to your unfailing love;
according to your great compassion blot out my transgressions.*
*² Wash away all my iniquity and cleanse me from my sin.*

**A Prayer for Deliverance from Adversaries**
    – Psalm 54:1-7
*¹ Save me, O God, by your name; vindicate me by your might.*
*² Hear my prayer, O God; listen to the words of my mouth.*

*³Arrogant foes are attacking me; ruthless people are trying to kill me—people without regard for God.*

**A Prayer for Retribution - Psalm 79:1-13**
*⁶Pour out your wrath on the nations that do not acknowledge you, on the kingdoms that do not call on your name*

**Prayer for Relief from Tormentors – Psalm 56:1-13**
*⁵All day long they twist my words; all their schemes are for my ruin. ⁶They conspire, they lurk, they watch my steps, hoping to take my life. ⁷Because of their wickedness do not let them escape; in your anger, God, bring the nations down.*

**Prayer for Safety from Enemies – Psalm 57:1-11**
*¹Have mercy on me, my God, have mercy on me, for in you I take refuge. I will take refuge in the shadow of your wings until the disaster has passed.*

**Urgent Prayer for the Restored Favor of God – Psalm 60:1-12**
*¹You have rejected us, God, and burst upon us; you have been angry—now restore us!*

**Prayer for Relief – Psalm 70:1-5**
*¹Hasten, O God, to save me; come quickly, LORD, to help me.*

**Prayer for Israel's Restoration – Psalm 80:1-19**
*¹Hear us, Shepherd of Israel, you who lead Joseph like a flock. You who sit enthroned between the cherubim, shine forth*

**Prayer to Frustrate Conspiracy – Psalm 83:1-18**
*¹O God, do not remain silent; do not turn a deaf ear, do not stand aloof, O God. ²See how your enemies growl, how your foes rear their heads. ³With cunning they conspire against your people; they plot against those you cherish.*

**Prayer that the Lord Will Restore Favor to the Land**
     **– Psalm 85:1-13**
*⁴Restore us again, God our Savior, and put away your displeasure toward us.*

*⁷Show us your unfailing love, LORD, and grant us your salvation.*

**Prayer for Mercy** – Psalm 86:1-17
*¹Hear me, LORD, and answer me, for I am poor and needy.
²Guard my life, for I am faithful to you; save your servant who trusts in you. You are my God; ³have mercy on me, Lord, for I call to you all day long. ⁴Bring joy to your servant, Lord, for I put my trust in you.*

**A Prayer for Help in Despondency** – Psalm 88:1-18
*³I am overwhelmed with troubles and my life draws near to death. ⁴I am counted among those who go down to the pit; I am like one without strength.*

**Prayer for Relief from Contempt** – Psalm 123:1-4
*³Have mercy on us, LORD, have mercy on us, for we have endured no end of contempt. ⁴We have endured no end of ridicule from the arrogant, of contempt from the proud.*

**Prayer for Deliverance from Evil Men** – Psalm 140:1-13
*¹Rescue me, LORD, from evildoers; protect me from the violent,
²who devise evil plans in their hearts and stir up war every day.*

**Prayer for Safekeeping from Wickedness** – Psalm 141:1-10
*⁸But my eyes are fixed on you, Sovereign LORD; in you I take refuge—do not give me over to death. ⁹Keep me safe from the traps set by evildoers, from the snares they have laid for me.
¹⁰Let the wicked fall into their own nets, while I pass by in safety.*

**A Prayer in Deep Distress** – Isaiah 33:1-9
*²LORD, be gracious to us; we long for you. Be our strength every morning, our salvation in time of distress.*

**Jeremiah Prays for Deliverance** – Jeremiah 17:14-18
*¹⁴Heal me, LORD, and I will be healed; save me and I will be saved, for you are the one I praise.
¹⁸Let my persecutors be put to shame, but keep me from shame; let them be terrified, but keep me from terror. Bring on them the day of disaster; destroy them with double destruction.*

**Nothing too Hard for the Lord** – Jeremiah 32:16-25
*17 Ah, Sovereign LORD, you have made the heavens and the earth by your great power and outstretched arm. Nothing is too hard for you.*

**Jeremiah's Prayer** – Jeremiah 10:23-25
*23 LORD, I know that people's lives are not their own; it is not for them to direct their steps. 24 Discipline me, LORD, but only in due measure— not in your anger, or you will reduce me to nothing.*

**A Prayer for Restoration** – Lamentations 5:1-22
*1 Remember, LORD, what has happened to us; look, and see our disgrace. 4 We must buy the water we drink; our wood can be had only at a price. 5 Those who pursue us are at our heels; we are weary and find no rest.*

**Daniel's Prayer for the People** – Daniel 9:19
*19 Lord, listen! Lord, forgive! Lord, hear and act! For your sake, my God, do not delay*

**Jonah's Prayer and Deliverance** – Jonah 1:17 - 2:10
*2 In my distress I called to the LORD, and he answered me. From deep in the realm of the dead I called for help, and you listened to my cry.*

**Prayer for God to Repeat His Deeds in Our Day**
        – Habakkuk 3:1-16
*2 LORD, I have heard of your fame; I stand in awe of your deeds, LORD. Repeat them in our day, in our time make them known; in wrath remember mercy.*

**The Lord's Prayer** – Matthew 6:5-15
*9 Our Father in heaven, hallowed be your name, 10 your kingdom come, your will be done, on earth as it is in heaven. 11 Give us today our daily bread. 12 And forgive us our debts, as we also have forgiven our debtors. 13 And lead us not into temptation but deliver us from the evil one.*

**Garden of Gethsemane Prayer** – Mark 14:32-42

³⁶ *"Abba, Father," he said, "everything is possible for you. Take this cup from me. Yet not what I will, but what you will."*

**Forgiveness and Prayer** – Mark 11:25-26
²⁵ *And when you stand praying, if you hold anything against anyone, forgive them, so that your Father in heaven may forgive you your sins.*

**Praying in the Name of Jesus** – John 14:12-14
¹² *Very truly I tell you, whoever believes in me will do the works I have been doing, and they will do even greater things than these, because I am going to the Father. ¹³ And I will do whatever you ask in my name, so that the Father may be glorified in the Son. ¹⁴ You may ask me for anything in my name, and I will do it.*

**Jesus Prays for Himself** – John 17:1-5
¹ *Father, the hour has come. Glorify your Son, that your Son may glorify you.*

**Jesus Prays for His Disciples** – John 17:6-19
¹⁵ *My prayer is not that you take them out of the world but that you protect them from the evil one.*

**Jesus Prays for All Believers** – John 17:20-26
²⁴ *Father, I want those you have given Me to be with Me where I am, and to see My glory, the glory you have given Me because you loved Me before the creation of the world.*

**The Upper Room Prayer Meetings** – Acts 1:12-14
¹⁴ *They all joined together constantly in prayer, along with the women and Mary the mother of Jesus, and with his brothers.*

**Prayer for Boldness** – Acts 4:23-31
²⁹ *Now, Lord, consider their threats and enable your servants to speak your word with great boldness. ³⁰ Stretch out your hand to heal and perform signs and wonders through the name of your holy servant Jesus. ³¹ After they prayed, the place where they were meeting was shaken. And they were all filled with the Holy Spirit and spoke the word of God boldly.*

**Prayer for Spiritual Wisdom** – Ephesians 1:15-23
*17 I keep asking that the God of our Lord Jesus Christ, the glorious Father, may give you the Spirit of wisdom and revelation, so that you may know him better. 18 I pray that the eyes of your heart may be enlightened in order that you may know the hope to which he has called you, the riches of his glorious inheritance in his holy people, 19 and his incomparably great power for us who believe.*

**A Prayer for Loved Ones** – Philippians 1:3-11
*9 And this is my prayer: that your love may abound more and more in knowledge and depth of insight, 10 so that you may be able to discern what is best and may be pure and blameless for the day of Christ, 11 filled with the fruit of righteousness that comes through Jesus Christ—to the glory and praise of God.*

**Prayer for the Church** – 1 Thessalonians 3:11-13
*13 May He strengthen your hearts so that you will be blameless and holy in the presence of our God and Father when our Lord Jesus comes with all his holy ones.*

**Confidence and Compassion in Prayer** – 1 John 5:14-17
*14 This is the confidence we have in approaching God: that if we ask anything according to his will, he hears us. 15 And if we know that he hears us—whatever we ask—we know that we have what we asked of him.*

**Prayer for Spiritual Strength** – Ephesians 3:14-21
*14 For this reason I kneel before the Father, 15 from whom every family[a] in heaven and on earth derives its name. 16 I pray that out of his glorious riches he may strengthen you with power through his Spirit in your inner being, 17 so that Christ may dwell in your hearts through faith. And I pray that you, being rooted and established in love, 18 may have power, together with all the Lord's holy people, to grasp how wide and long and high and deep is the love of Christ, 19 and to know this love that surpasses knowledge—that you may be filled to the measure of all the fullness of God.*

# HEALING

**Jesus Heals the Sick** - Matthew 4:23-25
*24 and people brought to him all who were ill with various diseases, those suffering severe pain, the demon-possessed, those having seizures, and the paralyzed; and he healed them.*

**The Faith of the Centurion** - Matthew 8:5-13
*13 Then Jesus said to the centurion, "Go! Let it be done just as you believed it would." And his servant was healed at that moment.*

**Peter's Mother-in-Law Healed** - Matthew 8:14-15
*14 When Jesus came into Peter's house, he saw Peter's mother-in-law lying in bed with a fever. 15 He touched her hand and the fever left her, and she got up and began to wait on him.*

**Many were healed** - Matthew 8:16-17
*16 When evening came, many who were demon-possessed were brought to him, and he drove out the spirits with a word and healed all the sick.*

**Men Healed of Demons** - Matthew 8:28-34
*32 He said to them (the demons), "Go!" So they came out and went into the pigs, and the whole herd rushed down the steep bank into the lake and died in the water.*

**A Paralytic is Healed** - Matthew 9:1-8
*6 So he said to the paralyzed man, "Get up, take your mat and go home." 7 Then the man got up and went home.*

**A Woman is Healed of a Bleeding Disorder** - Matthew 9:20-22
*21 She said to herself, "If I only touch his cloak, I will be healed." 22 Jesus turned and saw her. "Take heart, daughter," he said, "your faith has healed you." And the woman was healed at that moment.*

**Jesus Restores a Girl to Life - Matthew 9:23-25**
*23 When Jesus entered the synagogue leader's house and saw the noisy crowd and people playing pipes, 24 he said, "Go away. The girl is not dead but asleep." But they laughed at him. 25 After the crowd had been put outside, he went in and took the girl by the hand, and she got up.*

**Two Blind Men Healed - Matthew 9:27-31**
*29 Then he touched their eyes and said, "According to your faith let it be done to you"; 30 and their sight was restored.*

**A Man Healed of a Shriveled Hand - Matthew 12:9-14**
*13 Then he said to the man, "Stretch out your hand." So he stretched it out and it was completely restored, just as sound as the other.*

**Jesus Heals Great Multitudes - Matthew 15:29-31**
*30 Great crowds came to him, bringing the lame, the blind, the crippled, the mute and many others, and laid them at his feet; and he healed them.*

**Jesus Heals a Demon-possessed Boy - Matthew 17:14-21**
*18 Jesus rebuked the demon, and it came out of the boy, and he was healed at that moment.*

**God Heals Abimelek and his Family – Genesis 20:1-17**
*17 God healed Abimelek, his wife and his female slaves so they could have children again*

**Many Healed After Sabbath Sunset - Mark 1:32-34**
*34 and Jesus healed many who had various diseases. He also drove out many demons*

**Jesus Heals a Deaf-Mute - Mark 7:31-37**
*35 At this, the man's ears were opened, his tongue was loosened and he began to speak plainly.*

**A Blind Man Healed at Bethsaida** - Mark 8:22-26
*25 ... his eyes were opened, his sight was restored, and he saw everything clearly.*

**Jesus Heals Blind Bartimaeus** - Mark 10:46-52
*52 "Go," said Jesus, "your faith has healed you." Immediately he received his sight and followed Jesus along the road.*

**A Man with Dropsy Healed** - Luke 14:1-6
*4 So taking hold of the man, he healed him and sent him on his way.*

**A Nobleman's Son Healed** - John 4:46-54
*49 The royal official said, "Sir, come down before my child dies."50 "Go," Jesus replied, "your son will live."*

**A Man Healed at the Pool of Bethesda** - John 5:1-15
*6 When Jesus saw him lying there and learned that he had been in this condition for a long time, he asked him, "Do you want to get well?" 7 "Sir," the invalid replied, "I have no one to help me into the pool when the water is stirred. While I am trying to get in, someone else goes down ahead of me." 9 At once the man was cured; he picked up his mat and walked.*

**Peter Heals the Lame Man** - Acts 3:1-10
*8 Then Peter said to him, "Silver and gold I do not have, but what I do have I give you: In the name of Jesus Christ of Nazareth, rise up and walk."*

**Peter Heals Aeneas at Lydda** - Acts 9:32-35
*34 "Aeneas," Peter said to him, "Jesus Christ heals you. Get up and roll up your mat." Immediately Aeneas got up.*

**Peter raises Tabitha at Joppa** - Acts 9:36-42
*40 Peter sent them all out of the room; then he got down on his knees and prayed. Turning toward the dead woman, he said, "Tabitha, get up." She opened her eyes and seeing Peter she sat up. 41 He took her by the hand and helped her to her feet. Then he*

*called for the believers, especially the widows, and presented her
to them alive.*

**I am the LORD, who heals you** - Exodus 15:25-26
*26 He said, "If you listen carefully to the LORD your God and do
what is right in his eyes, if you pay attention to his commands
and keep all his decrees, I will not bring on you any of the
diseases I brought on the Egyptians, for I am the LORD, who
heals you."*

**Miriam is healed of leprosy** - Numbers 12:1-15
*13 So Moses cried out to the LORD, "Please, God, heal her!"*

**Healing of the Water -** 2 Kings 2:19-21
*21 Then he went out to the spring and threw the salt into it,
saying, "This is what the LORD says: 'I have healed this water.
Never again will it cause death or make the land unproductive.'"*

**Elisha Raises the Shunamite's Son** – 2 Kings 4:8-37
*32 When Elisha reached the house, there was the boy lying dead
on his couch. 33 He went in, shut the door on the two of them and
prayed to the LORD. 34 Then he got on the bed and lay on the boy,
mouth to mouth, eyes to eyes, hands to hands. As he
stretched himself out on him, the boy's body grew warm. 35 Elisha
turned away and walked back and forth in the room and then got
on the bed and stretched out on him once more. The boy sneezed
seven times and opened his eyes.*

**Naaman's Leprosy Healed -** 2 Kings 5:1-19
*14 So he went down and dipped himself in the Jordan seven
times, as the man of God had told him, and his flesh was
restored and became clean like that of a young boy.*

**Hezekiah is healed -** 2 Kings 20:1-11
*5 "Go back and tell Hezekiah, the ruler of my people, 'This is
what the LORD, the God of your father David, says: I have
heard your prayer and seen your tears; I will heal you.*

**I will forgive their sin and will heal their land**
        - 2 Chronicles 7:13-14
*14 if my people, who are called by my name, will
humble themselves and pray and seek my face and turn from
their wicked ways, then I will hear from heaven, and I will
forgive their sin and will heal their land.*

**Hezekiah Prays for the People -** 2 Chronicles 30:18-20
*20 And the LORD heard Hezekiah and healed the people.*

**David is Healed -** Psalm 30:1-3
*2 LORD my God, I called to you for help, and you healed me.*

**God Heals Those Who Regard the Weak -** Psalm 41:1-4
*1 Blessed are those who have regard for the weak;
the LORD delivers them in times of trouble.*

**The Lord Heals Us -** Psalm 103:1-5
*2 Praise the Lord, my soul, and forget not all His benefits - 3 who
forgives all your sins and heals all your diseases*

**God Heals the Foolish and Rebellious -** Psalm 107:17-20
*17 Some became fools through their rebellious ways and suffered
affliction because of their iniquities. 19 Then they cried to
the LORD in their trouble, and he saved them from their
distress. 20 He sent out his word and healed them; he
rescued them from the grave.*

**God Heals the Brokenhearted -** Psalm 147:3
*3 He heals the brokenhearted and binds up their wounds.*

**By His Wounds We Are Healed -** Isaiah 53:5
*5 But he was pierced for our transgressions, he was crushed for
our iniquities; the punishment that brought us peace was on
him, and by his wounds we are healed.*

**Healing for the Backslider -** Isaiah 57:14-21
*18 I have seen their ways, but I will heal them; I will guide them
and restore comfort*

**Healing for Those Who Revere God's Name -** Malachi 4:2

*² But for you who revere my name, the sun of righteousness will rise with healing in its rays. And you will go out and frolic like well-fed calves.*

# WISDOM

**How Wisdom Begins** - Psalm 111:10
*[10] The fear of the LORD is the beginning of wisdom; all who follow his precepts have good understanding. To him belongs eternal praise.*

**Wisdom is from God** - Proverbs 2:6
*[6] For the LORD gives wisdom; from his mouth come knowledge and understanding.*

**Ask for Wisdom** - James 1:5
*[5] If any of you lacks wisdom, you should ask God, who gives generously to all without finding fault, and it will be given to you.*

**Wisdom is Profitable** - Proverbs 3:13-14
*[13] Blessed are those who find wisdom, those who gain understanding, [14] for she is more profitable than silver and yields better returns than gold.*

**Works of Wisdom** - Proverbs 3:19-20
*[19] By wisdom the LORD laid the earth's foundations, by understanding he set the heavens in place; [20] by his knowledge the watery depths were divided, and the clouds let drop the dew.*

**Wisdom is from the Beginning** - Proverbs 8:22
*[22] "The LORD brought me forth as the first of his works, before his deeds of old;*

**Wisdom Brings Life** - Proverbs 3:21-22
*[21] My son, do not let wisdom and understanding out of your sight, preserve sound judgment and discretion; [22] they will be life for you, an ornament to grace your neck.*

**Wisdom's Protection** - Proverbs 4:6
*6 Do not forsake wisdom, and she will protect you; love her, and she will watch over you.*

**With Humility Comes Wisdom** - Proverbs 11:2
*2 When pride comes, then comes disgrace, but with humility comes wisdom.*

**Wisdom's Instruction** - Proverbs 15:33
*33 Wisdom's instruction is to fear the LORD, and humility comes before honor.*

**God's Wisdom** - Romans 11:33-36
*33 Oh, the depth of the riches of the wisdom and knowledge of God! How unsearchable his judgments, and his paths beyond tracing out! 34 "Who has known the mind of the Lord? Or who has been his counselor?" 35 "Who has ever given to God, that God should repay them?" 36 For from him and through him and for him are all things. To him be the glory forever! Amen.*

**Wisdom a Mystery** - 1 Corinthians 2:7
*7 No, we declare God's wisdom, a mystery that has been hidden and that God destined for our glory before time began.*

**Worldly Wisdom** - 1 Corinthians 3:18-19
*18 Do not deceive yourselves. If any of you think you are wise by the standards of this age, you should become "fools" so that you may become wise. 19 For the wisdom of this world is foolishness in God's sight. As it is written: "He catches the wise in their craftiness"*

**Living With Wisdom** - Ephesians 5:15-17
*15 Be very careful, then, how you live—not as unwise but as wise, 16 making the most of every opportunity, because the days are evil. 17 Therefore do not be foolish, but understand what the Lord's will is.*

**Solomon Requests Wisdom Above all Else** – 1 Kings 3:1-15
*7 "Now, LORD my God, you have made your servant king in place of my father David. But I am only a little child and do not know how to carry out my duties. 8 Your servant is here among the people you have chosen, a great people, too numerous to count or number. 9 So give your servant a discerning heart to govern your people and to distinguish between right and wrong. For who is able to govern this great people of yours?"*

**Solomon's Wisdom** – 1 Kings 4:29-34
*29 God gave Solomon wisdom and very great insight, and a breadth of understanding as measureless as the sand on the seashore. 30 Solomon's wisdom was greater than the wisdom of all the people of the East, and greater than all the wisdom of Egypt.*

**Prayer for Spiritual Wisdom** – Ephesians 1:15-23
*17 I keep asking that the God of our Lord Jesus Christ, the glorious Father, may give you the Spirit of wisdom and revelation, so that you may know him better. 18 I pray that the eyes of your heart may be enlightened in order that you may know the hope to which he has called you, the riches of his glorious inheritance in his holy people, 19 and his incomparably great power for us who believe.*

**A Heart of Wisdom** - Psalm 90:12
*So teach us to number our days, that we may gain a heart of wisdom.*

**Wisdom Keeps Us on a Straight Path** - Proverbs 15:21
*21 Folly brings joy to one who has no sense, but whoever has understanding keeps a straight course.*

**Wisdom Brings Peace** - Proverbs 29:11
*11 Fools give full vent to their rage, but the wise bring calm in the end.*

**Wisdom Gives Discernment** - Proverbs 14:8
*8 The wisdom of the prudent is to give thought to their ways, but the folly of fools is deception.*

**The Call of Wisdom** – Proverbs 1:20-33
[20] *Out in the open wisdom calls aloud, she raises her voice in the public square; [21] on top of the wall[a] she cries out, at the city gate she makes her speech:*

**The Value of Wisdom** - Proverbs 2:1-22
[12] *Wisdom will save you from the ways of wicked men, from men whose words are perverse, [13] who have left the straight paths to walk in dark ways, [14] who delight in doing wrong and rejoice in the perverseness of evil, [15] whose paths are crooked and who are devious in their ways.*

**Wisdom Bestows Well-Being** – Proverbs 3:1-35
[1] *My son, do not forget my teaching, but keep my commands in your heart, [2] for they will prolong your life many years and bring you peace and prosperity.*

**Security in Wisdom** - Proverbs 4:1-27
[6] *Do not forsake wisdom, and she will protect you; love her, and she will watch over you.*

**The Excellence of Wisdom** - Proverbs 8:1-36
[5] *You who are simple, gain prudence; you who are foolish, set your hearts on it. [6] Listen, for I have trustworthy things to say; I open my lips to speak what is right.*

**The Invitation of Wisdom** - Proverbs 9:1-18
[3] *She has sent out her servants, and she calls from the highest point of the city, "Let all who are simple come to my house!"*

**The Wisdom of Agur** - Proverbs 30:1-33
[5] *Every word of God is flawless; he is a shield to those who take refuge in him. [6] Do not add to his words, or he will rebuke you and prove you a liar.*

**Listen to Wisdom** - Ecclesiastes 7:5
[5] *It is better to heed the rebuke of a wise person than to listen to the song of fools.*

**Wisdom Better than Weapons** - Ecclesiastes 9:17-18
*<sup>17</sup> The quiet words of the wise are more to be heeded than the shouts of a ruler of fools. <sup>18</sup> Wisdom is better than weapons of war, but one sinner destroys much good.*

**Christ the Power and Wisdom of God** - Ecclesiastes 1:18-2:5
*<sup>19</sup> For it is written: "I will destroy the wisdom of the wise; the intelligence of the intelligent I will frustrate."*

**Spiritual Wisdom** - 1 Corinthians 2:6-16
*<sup>13</sup> This is what we speak, not in words taught us by human wisdom but in words taught by the Spirit, explaining spiritual realities with Spirit-taught words.*

**Prayer for Spiritual Wisdom** - Ephesians 1:15-23
*<sup>17</sup> I keep asking that the God of our Lord Jesus Christ, the glorious Father, may give you the Spirit of wisdom and revelation, so that you may know him better.*

**Godly Wisdom and Demonic Wisdom** - James 3:13-18
*<sup>17</sup> But the wisdom that comes from heaven is first of all pure; then peace-loving, considerate, submissive, full of mercy and good fruit, impartial and sincere.*

# FAITH

**Faith in God, Not Ourselves** - Proverbs 3:5-6
*[5] Trust in the LORD with all your heart and lean not on your own understanding; [6] in all your ways submit to him, and he will make your paths straight.*

**Abraham Justified by Faith** – Romans 4:1-4
*[3] "Abraham believed God, and it was credited to him as righteousness."*

**Faithful Abraham** – Hebrews 11:8-12
*[8] By faith Abraham, when called to go to a place he would later receive as his inheritance, obeyed and went, even though he did not know where he was going.*

**Faith is a Shield** - 1 Peter 1:5
*[5] Through faith we are shielded by God's power until the coming of the salvation that is ready to be revealed in the last time.*

**Noah Pleases God By Faithfulness** – Genesis 6:1-12
*[9] Noah was a righteous man, blameless among the people of his time, and he walked faithfully with God.*

**A Prayer for Faith in Time of Distress** – Psalm 6:1-10
*[2] Have mercy on me, LORD, for I am faint; heal me, LORD, for my bones are in agony.*

**Reliance on God's Faithfulness** – Psalm 26:1-12
*[2] Test me, LORD, and try me, examine my heart and my mind; [3] for I have always been mindful of your unfailing love and have lived in reliance on your faithfulness.*

**Faith in Time of Trouble** – Psalm 43:1-5
*[3] Send me your light and your faithful care, let them lead me; let them bring me to your holy mountain, to the place where you dwell.*

**Faith for Mercy** – Psalm 86:1-17
*[1] Hear me, LORD, and answer me, for I am poor and needy.
[2] Guard my life, for I am faithful to you; save your servant who
trusts in you. You are my God; [3] have mercy on me, Lord, for I
call to you all day long. [4] Bring joy to your servant, Lord, for I
put my trust in you.*

**The Faith of the Centurion** - Matthew 8:5-13
*[13] Then Jesus said to the centurion, "Go! Let it be done just as
you believed it would." And his servant was healed at that
moment.*

**Faith for Healing** - Matthew 9:20-22
*[21] She said to herself, "If I only touch his cloak, I will be healed."
[22] Jesus turned and saw her. "Take heart, daughter," he said,
"your faith has healed you." And the woman was healed at that
moment.*

**According to Your Faith** - Matthew 9:27-31
*[29] Then he touched their eyes and said, "According to your faith
let it be done to you"; [30] and their sight was restored.*

**Your Faith Has Healed You** - Mark 10:46-52
*[52] "Go," said Jesus, "your faith has healed you." Immediately he
received his sight and followed Jesus along the road.*

**Safety of the Faithful** - Psalm 4:1-8
*[8] In peace I will lie down and sleep, for you alone, LORD,
make me dwell in safety.*

**Faith in the LORD** - Psalm 11:1-7
*[4] The LORD is in his holy temple; the LORD is on his heavenly
throne. He observes everyone on earth; his eyes examine them.*

**The Hope of the Faithful** - Psalm 16:1-11
*[5] LORD, you alone are my portion and my cup; you make my
lot secure. [6] The boundary lines have fallen for me in pleasant
places; surely I have a delightful inheritance. [7] I will praise
the LORD, who counsels me; even at night my heart instructs me.*

*⁸ I keep my eyes always on the LORD. With him at my right hand, I will not be shaken.*

**Declaration of Faith** - Psalm 27:1-14
*¹ The LORD is my light and my salvation— whom shall I fear? The LORD is the stronghold of my life— of whom shall I be afraid?*

**Faith Rewarded** - Psalm 40:1-17
*¹ I waited patiently for the LORD; he turned to me and heard my cry.*
*⁴ Blessed is the one who trusts in the LORD, who does not look to the proud, to those who turn aside to false gods.*

**Faith in the LORD's Goodness** - Psalm 138:1-8
*⁷ Though I walk in the midst of trouble, you preserve my life. You stretch out your hand against the anger of my foes; with your right hand you save me.*

**Faith of the Canaanite Woman** – Matthew 15:21-28
*²⁸ Then Jesus said to her, "Woman, you have great faith! Your request is granted." And her daughter was healed at that moment.*

**Mustard Seed Faith** - Luke 17:1-10
*⁶ He replied, "If you have faith as small as a mustard seed, you can say to this mulberry tree, 'Be uprooted and planted in the sea,' and it will obey you."*

**Justified Through Faith** - Romans 5:1-11
*¹ Therefore, since we have been justified through faith, we have peace with God through our Lord Jesus Christ, ² through whom we have gained access by faith into this grace in which we now stand. And we boast in the hope of the glory of God.*

**Children of Abraham by Faith** - Galatians 3:1-14
*⁷ Understand, then, that those who have faith are children of Abraham.*

**Colossal Faith** - Colossians 1:3-14

*³ We always thank God, the Father of our Lord Jesus Christ, when we pray for you, ⁴ because we have heard of your faith in Christ Jesus and of the love you have for all God's people— ⁵ the faith and love that spring from the hope stored up for you in heaven and about which you have already heard in the true message of the gospel ⁶ that has come to you.*

**Work Produced by Faith** - 1 Thessalonians 1:2-10

*³ We remember before our God and Father your work produced by faith,*

**Hold Fast to Your Faith** - Hebrews 10:19-39

*²² let us draw near to God with a sincere heart and with the full assurance that faith brings, having our hearts sprinkled to cleanse us from a guilty conscience and having our bodies washed with pure water. ²³ Let us hold unswervingly to the hope we profess, for he who promised is faithful.*

**Faith in Action** – Hebrews 11:1- 40

*³ By faith we understand that the universe was formed at God's command, so that what is seen was not made out of what was visible.*
*⁵ By faith Enoch was taken from this life, so that he did not experience death: "He could not be found, because God had taken him away."*
*⁷ By faith Noah, when warned about things not yet seen, in holy fear built an ark to save his family.*
*⁸ By faith Abraham, when called to go to a place he would later receive as his inheritance, obeyed and went, even though he did not know where he was going.*
*¹⁷ By faith Abraham, when God tested him, offered Isaac as a sacrifice.*
*²⁴ By faith Moses, when he had grown up, refused to be known as the son of Pharaoh's daughter.*
*²⁹ By faith the people passed through the Red Sea as on dry land*
*³⁰ By faith the walls of Jericho fell*

**Jesus, the Perfecter of Faith** - Hebrews 11:1-12:3
*¹Therefore, since we are surrounded by such a great cloud of witnesses, let us throw off everything that hinders and the sin that so easily entangles. And let us run with perseverance the race marked out for us, ²fixing our eyes on Jesus, the pioneer and perfecter of faith.*

**Faith Without Works Is Dead** - James 2:14-26
*¹⁴What good is it, my brothers and sisters, if someone claims to have faith but has no deeds?*
*²⁶As the body without the spirit is dead, so faith without deeds is dead.*

**The Prayer of Faith** - James 5:13-20
*¹⁵And the prayer offered in faith will make the sick person well; the Lord will raise them up. If they have sinned, they will be forgiven.*

**Growing in the Faith** – 2 Peter 1:3-11
*⁵For this very reason, make every effort to add to your faith goodness; and to goodness, knowledge; ⁶and to knowledge, self-control; and to self-control, perseverance; and to perseverance, godliness; ⁷and to godliness, mutual affection; and to mutual affection, love.*

**Faith Overcomes the World** – 1 John 5:1-12
*⁵Who is it that overcomes the world? Only the one who believes that Jesus is the Son of God.*

**Faith Can Move Mountains** – Mark 11:23
*²³"Truly I tell you, if anyone says to this mountain, 'Go, throw yourself into the sea,' and does not doubt in their heart but believes that what they say will happen, it will be done for them.*

**Have Faith Instead of Doubt** - James 1:6
*⁶But when you ask, you must believe and not doubt, because the one who doubts is like a wave of the sea, blown and tossed by the wind.*

**Have Faith, Not Fear** - Isaiah 43:1-7

*¹ "Do not fear, for I have redeemed you; I have summoned you by name; you are mine.² When you pass through the waters,  I will be with you; and when you pass through the rivers, they will not sweep over you. When you walk through the fire, you will not be burned; the flames will not set you ablaze.³ For I am the LORD your God, the Holy One of Israel, your Savior;*

**Faith Works** - Psalm 37:5

*⁵ Commit your way to the LORD; trust in him and he will do this:*

**Faith for Future Joy** - Romans 8:18

*"The pain that you've been feeling, can't compare to the joy that's coming."*

**Faith of the Virtuous Woman** - Proverbs 31:10-31

*²⁵ "She is clothed in strength, and dignity, and she laughs without fear of the future."*

**Live by Faith - 2 Corinthians 5:6-7**

*⁶ Therefore we are always confident and know that as long as we are at home in the body we are away from the Lord. ⁷ For we live by faith, not by sight.*

**The Shield of Faith -** Ephesians 6:16

*¹⁶ In addition to all this, take up the shield of faith, with which you can extinguish all the flaming arrows of the evil one.*

**Faith Brings Safety** - Proverbs 29:25

*²⁵ Fear of man will prove to be a snare, but whoever trusts in the LORD is kept safe.*

**Have Faith, Not Timidity** - 2 Timothy 1:7

*⁷ For the Spirit God gave us does not make us timid, but gives us power, love and self-discipline.*

# PARABLES

**The Parable of the Trees** – Judges 9:7-21
**Nathan's Parable About David** – 2 Samuel 12:1-15
**The Parable of the Sower**
    – Matthew 13:1-9, Mark 4:1-9 and Luke 8:4-8
**The Parable of the Sower Explained**
    – Matthew 13:18-23, Mark 4:10-20 and Luke 8:11-15
**The Purpose of Parables**
    – Matthew 13:10-17, Mark 4:10-12 and Luke 8:9-10
**The Parable of the Weeds** – Matthew 13:24-29
**The Parable of the Weeds Explained** – Matthew 13:36-43
**The Parables of the Mustard Seed and the Yeast**
    – Matthew 13:31-35, Mark 4:30-32 and Luke 13:18-19
**The Parables of the Hidden Treasure and the Pearl**
    – Matthew 13:44-46
**The Parable of the Dragnet** – Matthew 13:47-52
**The Parable of the Lost Sheep**
    – Matthew 18:10-14 and Luke 15:1-7
**The Parable of the Unmerciful Servant** – Matthew 18:21-35
**The Parable of the Workers in the Vineyard**
    – Matthew 20:1-16
**The Parable of the Two Sons** – Matthew 21:28-32
**The Parable of the Tenants**
    – Matthew 21:33-46, Mark 12:1-12, Luke 20:9-19
**The Parable of the Wedding Feast** – Matthew 22:1-14
**The Parable of the Fig Tree**
    – Matthew 24:32-35, Mark 13:28-31, Luke 21:29-33
**The Parable of the Ten Virgins** – Matthew 25:1-13
**The Parable of the Talents** – Matthew 25:14-30
**The Parable of the Growing Seed** – Mark 4:26-29
**Jesus' Use of Parables** – Mark 4:33-34
**The Parable of a Lamp on a Stand** – Luke 8:16-18
**The Parable of the Good Samaritan** – Luke 10:25-37
**The Parable of the Rich Fool** – Luke 12:13-21
**The Parable of the Great Banquet** – Luke 14:15-24
**The Parable of the Lost Coin** – Luke 15:8-10
**The Parable of the Prodigal Son** – Luke 15:11-32
**The Parable of the Shrewd Manager** – Luke 16:1-13

**The Parable of the Persistent Widow** – Luke 18:1-8
**The Parable of the Pharisee and the Tax Collector**
    – Luke 18:9-14
**The Parable of the Ten Minas** – Luke 19:11-27

# VISIONS

**Ezekiel's Vision of God** – Ezekiel 1:1-28
**Vision of the Four Beasts** – Daniel 7:1-8
**Vision of the Ancient of Days** – Daniel 7:9-14
**Daniel's Vision Interpreted** – Daniel 7:15-28
**Vision of a Ram and a Goat** – Daniel 8:1-14
**Gabriel Interprets the Vision** – Daniel 8:15-27
**Vision of the Glorious Man** – Daniel 10:1-9
**Vision of the Locusts** – Amos 7:1-3
**Vision of the Fire** – Amos 7:4-6
**Vision of the Plumb Line** – Amos 7:7-9
**Vision of the Summer Fruit** – Amos 8:1-14
**Vision of the Horses** – Zechariah 1:7-11
**Vision of the Horns** – Zechariah 1:18-20
**Vision of the Measuring Line** – Zechariah 2:1-5
**Vision of the High Priest** – Zechariah 3:1-5
**Vision of The Coming Branch** – Zechariah3:6-10
**Vision of the Lampstand and Olive Trees** – Zechariah 4:1-14
**Vision of the Flying Scroll** – Zechariah 5:1-4
**Vision of the Woman in a Basket** – Zechariah 5:5-11
**Vision of the Four Chariots** – Zechariah 6:1-8
**Peter's Vision** – Acts 10:9-16
**The Vision of Paradise** – 2 Corinthians 12:1-6
**Vision of the Son of Man** – Revelation 1:9-20

# <u>PROPHECIES</u>

**The Seventy-Weeks Prophecy** – Daniel 9:20-27
**Prophecy of the End Time** – Daniel 12:1-13
**Prophecy Against Eli's Household** – 1 Samuel 2:22-36
**Samuel's First Prophecy** – 1 Samuel 3:1-21
**Balaam's First Prophecy** – Numbers 22:41 – 23:12
**Balaam's Second Prophecy** – Numbers 23:13-26
**Balaam's Third Prophecy** – Numbers 23:27 – 24:14
**Balaam's Fourth Prophecy** – Numbers 24:15-25
**Samuel's First Prophecy** – 1 Samuel 3:1-21
**The Immanuel Prophecy** – Isaiah 7:10-25
**Prophecies Concerning Persia and Greece**
    – Daniel 10:10 – 11:4
**Prophecy of the End Time** – Daniel 12:1-13
**Prophecy of the Shepherds** – Zechariah 11:4-17
**Prophecy and the Parables** – Matthew 13:34-35
**Zacharia's Prophecy** – Luke 1:67-80
**Prophecy and Tongues** – 1 Corinthians 14:1-5

# OLD TESTAMENT INDEX

## EXODUS

## LEVITICUS

## NUMBERS

Chapter 10:28-43
    - **Southern Cities Conquered**
Chapter 11:1-23
    - **Northern Kings Defeated**
Chapter 12:1-6
    - **List of Defeated Kings**
Chapter 13:1-7
    - **Remaining Land to Be Conquered**
Chapter 13:8-33
    - **Division of the Land East of the Jordan**
Chapter 14:1-5
    - **Division of the Land West of the Jordan**
Chapter 14:6-15
    - **Allotment for Caleb**
Chapter 15:1-12
    - **Allotment for Judah**
Chapter 16:1-17:18
    - **Allotment for Ephraim and Manasseh**
Chapter 18:1-10
    - **Division of the Rest of the Land**
Chapter 18:11-28
    - **Allotment for Benjamin**
Chapter 19:1-9
    - **Simeon's Inheritance with Judah**
Chapter 19:10-16
    - **The Land of Zebulun**
Chapter 19:17-23
    - **The Land of Issachar**
Chapter 19:24-31
    - **The Land of Asher**
Chapter 19:32-39
    - **The Land of Naphtali**
Chapter 19:40-48
    - **The Land of Dan**
Chapter 19:49-51
    - **Joshua's Inheritance**
Chapter 20:1-9
    - **The Cities of Refuge**
Chapter 21:1-42
    - **Towns for the Levites**
Chapter 22:1-9
    - **Eastern Tribes Return to Their Lands**

Chapter 23:1-16
        **- Joshua's Farewell to the Leaders**
Chapter 24:1-28
        **- The Covenant Renewed at Shechem**
Chapter 24:29-33
        **- Buried in the Promised Land**


<u>**JUDGES**</u>

Chapter 1:1-36
        **- The Continuing Conquest of Canaan**
Chapter 2:1-4
        **- The Angel of the Lord at Bokim**
Chapter 2:6-3:6
        **- Disobedience and Defeat**
Chapter 3:7-11
        **- Othniel**
Chapter 3:12-30
        **- Ehud**
Chapter 3:31
        **- Shamgar**
Chapter 4:1-24
        **Deborah**
Chapter 5:1-31
        **- The Song of Deborah**
Chapter 6:1-40
        **- Gideon**
Chapter 7:1-25
        **- Gideon's Valiant Three Hundred**
Chapter 8:1-21
        **- Zebah and Zalmunna**
Chapter 8:22-27
        **- Gideon's Ephod**
Chapter 8:28-35
        **- Death of Gideon**
Chapter 9:1-57
        **- Abimelek**
Chapter 10:1-2
        **- Tola**
Chapter 10:3-5
        **- Jair**

Chapter 4:18-22
    **- The Genealogy of David**


# 1 SAMUEL

Chapter 1:1-20
    **- The Birth of Samuel**
Chapter 1:20-28
    **- Hannah Dedicates Samuel**
Chapter 2:1-11
    **- Hannah's Prayer**
Chapter 2:12-26
    **- The Wicked Sons of Eli**
Chapter 2:27-36
    **- Prophecy Against Eli's Household**
Chapter 3:1-21
    **- The Lord Calls Samuel**
Chapter 4:1-11
    **- The Philistines Capture the Ark of God**
Chapter 4:12-22
    **- Death of Eli**
Chapter 5:1-12
    **- The Ark in Ashdod and Ekron**
Chapter 6:1-7:2
    **- The Ark Returned to Israel**
Chapter 7:2-17
    **- Samuel Subdues the Philistines at Mizpah**
Chapter 8:1-22
    **- Israel Asks for a King**
Chapter 9:1-10:8
    **- Samuel Anoints Saul**
Chapter 10:9-27
    **- Saul Made King**
Chapter 11:1-11
    **- Saul Saves Jabesh Gilead**
Chapter 11:12-15
    **- Saul Confirmed as King**
Chapter 12:1-25
    **- Samuel's Farewell Speech**
Chapter 13:1-15
    **- Samuel Rebukes Saul**

Chapter 23:1-7
  - **David's Last Words**
Chapter 23:8-39
  - **David's Mighty Warriors**
Chapter 24:1-17
  - **David Enrolls the Fighting Men**
Chapter 24:18-25
  - **David Builds an Altar on the Threshing Floor**


## <u>1 KINGS</u>

Chapter 1:1-27
  - **Adonijah Sets Himself Up as King**
Chapter 1:28-53
  - **David Proclaims Solomon King**
Chapter 2:1-12
  - **David's Charge to Solomon**
Chapter 2:13-46
  - **Solomon's Throne Established**
Chapter 3:1-15
  - **Solomon Asks for Wisdom**
Chapter 3:16-28
  - **Solomon's Wise Judgment**
Chapter 4:1-19
  - **Solomon's Administration**
Chapter 4:20-28
  - **Solomon's Daily Provisions**
Chapter 4:29-34
  - **Solomon's Wisdom**
Chapter 5:1-18
  - **Solomon Prepares to Build the Temple**
Chapter 6:1-38
  - **Solomon Builds the Temple**
Chapter 7:1-12
  - **Solomon Builds His Palace**
Chapter 7:13-51
  - **The Temple's Furnishings**
Chapter 8:1-21
  - **The Ark Brought into the Temple**
Chapter 8:22-61
  - **Solomon's Prayer of Dedication**

## 2 KINGS

## 1 CHRONICLES

## 2 CHRONICLES

## EZRA

## NEHEMIAH

Chapter 3:1-32
        - **Rebuilding the Wall**
Chapter 4:1-23
        - **Opposition to Rebuilding**
Chapter 5:1-19
        - **Nehemiah Deals with Oppression**
Chapter 6:1-15
        - **Conspiracy Against Nehemiah**
Chapter 6:16-7:3
        - **The Wall Completed**
Chapter 7:4-73
        - **The Captives Who Returned to Jerusalem**
Chapter 8:1-18
        - **Ezra Reads the Law**
Chapter 9:1-37
        - **The People Confess Their Sins**
Chapter 9:38-10:39
        - **The People Who Sealed the Covenant**
Chapter 11:1-36
        - **The New Residents of Jerusalem**
Chapter 12:1-26
        - **The Priests and Levites**
Chapter 12:27-47
        - **Nehemiah Dedicates the Wall**
Chapter 13:1-31
        - **Nehemiah's Final Reforms**


<u>**ESTHER**</u>

Chapter 1:1-22
        - **The King Dethrones Queen Vashti**
Chapter 2:1-18
        - **Esther Becomes Queen**
Chapter 2:19-23
        - **Mordecai Discovers a Plot**
Chapter 3:1-15
        - **Haman's Conspiracy Against the Jews**
Chapter 4:1-17
        - **Esther Agrees to Help the Jews**
Chapter 5:1-8
        - **Esther's Banquet**

## JOB

## PSALM

Chapter 69:1-36
        - **An Urgent Plea for Help in Trouble**
Chapter 70:1-5
        - **Prayer for Relief from Adversaries**
Chapter 71:1-24
        - **God the Rock of Salvation**
Chapter 72:1-20
        - **Glory and Universality of the Messiah's Reign**

   BOOK THREE: PSALMS 73 – 89
Chapter 73:1-28
        - **The Tragedy of the Wicked, and the Blessedness of Trust in God**
Chapter 74:1-23
        - **A Plea for Relief from Oppressors**
Chapter 75:1-10
        - **Thanksgiving for God's Righteous Judgment**
Chapter 76:1-12
        - **The Majesty of God in Judgment**
Chapter 77:1-20
        - **The Consoling Memory of God's Redemptive Works**
Chapter 78:1-72
        - **God's Kindness to Rebellious Israel**
Chapter 79:1-13
        - **A Dirge and a Prayer for Israel, Destroyed by Enemies**
Chapter 80:1-19
        - **Prayer for Israel's Restoration**
Chapter 81:1-16
        - **An Appeal for Israel's Repentance**
Chapter 82:1-8
        - **A Plea for Justice**
Chapter 83:1-18
        - **Prayer to Frustrate Conspiracy Against Israel**
Chapter 84:1-12
        - **The Blessedness of Dwelling in the House of God**
Chapter 85:1-13
        - **Prayer that the LORD Will Restore Favor to the Land**
Chapter 86:1-17
        - **Prayer for Mercy, with Meditation on the Excellencies of the LORD**
Chapter 87:1-7
        - **The Glories of the City of God**

## ECCLESIASTES

## JEREMIAH

## <u>LAMENTATIONS</u>

## HOSEA

Chapter 13:1-16
    **- The Lord's Anger Against Israel**
Chapter 14:1-9
    **- Repentance to Bring Blessing**


## JOEL

Chapter 1:1-12
    **- Invasion of Locusts**
Chapter 1:13-20
    **- Mourning for the Land**
Chapter 2:1-11
    **- The Day of the LORD**
Chapter 2:12-17
    **- A Call to Repentance**
Chapter 2:18-27
    **- The Land Refreshed**
Chapter 2:28-32
    **- God's Spirit Poured Out**
Chapter 3:1-16
    **- God Judges the Nations**
Chapter 3:17-21
    **- God Blesses His People**


## AMOS

Chapter 1:1-Chapter 2:5
    **- Judgment on the Israel's Neighbors**
Chapter 2:6-16
    **- Judgment on Israel**
Chapter 3:1-15
    **- Witnesses Summoned Against Israel**
Chapter 4:1-13
    **- Israel Did Not Accept Correction**
Chapter 5:1-17
    **- A Lament and Call to Repentance**
Chapter 5:18-27
    **- The Day of the LORD**
Chapter 6:1-7
    **- Warnings to the Complacent**

Chapter 2:12-13
- **Deliverance Promised**
Chapter 3:1-12
- **Wicked Rulers and Prophets**
Chapter 4:1-5
- **The Mountain of the LORD**
Chapter 4:6-13
- **The Lord's Plan**
Chapter 5:1-15
- **The Coming Messiah**
Chapter 6:1-8
- **The Lord's Case Against Israel**
Chapter 6:9-16
- **Israel's Guilt and Punishment**
Chapter 7:1-7
- **Sorrow for Israel's Sins**
Chapter 7:8-13
- **Israel's Confession and Comfort**
Chapter 7:14-20
- **Prayer and Praise**

## NAHUM

Chapter 1:1-15
- **God's Anger Against Nineveh**
Chapter 2:1-13
- **The Destruction of Nineveh**
Chapter 3:1-19
- **Woe to Nineveh**

## HABAKKUK

Chapter 1:1-4
- **Habakkuk's Complaint**
Chapter 1:5-11
- **The LORD's Reply**
Chapter 1:12-Chapter 2:1
- **The Prophet's Second Complaint**
Chapter 2:2-20
- **The Lord's Answer**
Chapter 3:1-19
- **Habakkuk's Prayer**

## MALACHI

# NEW TESTAMENT INDEX

## MATTHEW

## <u>MARK</u>

## LUKE

## <u>JOHN</u>

## <u>ACTS</u>

<u>**1 CORINTHIANS**</u>

Chapter 1:1-3
   **- Greeting**
Chapter 1:4-9
   **- Thankfulness**
Chapter 1:10-17
   **- Division Rebuked**
Chapter 1:18-2:5
   **- Christ the Power and Wisdom of God**
Chapter 2:6-16
   **- Spiritual Wisdom**
Chapter 3:1-23
   **- The Church and it's Leadership**
Chapter 4:1-13
   **- The Nature of True Apostleship**
Chapter 4:14-21
   **- Paul's Appeal and Warning**
Chapter 5:1-13
   **- Immorality Defiles the Church**
Chapter 6:1-11
   **- Do Not Sue the Brethren**
Chapter 6:12-20
   **- Glorify God in Body and Spirit**
Chapter 7:1-16
   **- Principles of Marriage**
Chapter 7:17-24
   **- Live as You Are Called**
Chapter 7:25-40
   **- To the Unmarried and Widows**
Chapter 8:1-13
   **- Food Sacrificed to Idols**
Chapter 9:1-18
   **- Rights as an Apostle**
Chapter 9:19-23
   **- Paul's Choice**
Chapter 9:24-27
   **- Self-Discipline**
Chapter 10:1-13
   **- Old Testament Examples**
Chapter 10:14-22
   **- Flee from Idolatry**
Chapter 10:23-33

## 2 CORINTHIANS

## <u>GALATIANS</u>

## EPHESIANS

Chapter 6:10-20
- **The Whole Armor of God**
Chapter 6:21-24
- **Final Greetings**


## PHILIPPIANS

Chapter 1:1-2
- **Greeting**
Chapter 1:3-11
- **Thankfulness and Prayer**
Chapter 1:12-26
- **Christ Is Preached Regardless of Chains**
Chapter 1:27-30
- **The Gospel is Worthy of Suffering**
Chapter 2:1-11
- **Unity Through Humility**
Chapter 2:12-18
- **Serve Without Grumbling**
Chapter 2:19-30
- **Timothy and Epaphroditus**
Chapter 3:1-14
- **Pressing Toward the Goal**
Chapter 3:15-4:3
- **Following Paul's Example**
Chapter 4:4-9
- **Final Exhortations**
Chapter 4:10-20
- **Philippian Generosity**
Chapter 4:21-23
- **Final Greetings and Blessing**


## COLOSSIANS

Chapter 1:1-2
- **Greeting**
Chapter 1:3-14
- **Faith in Christ**
Chapter 1:15-23
- **Supremacy of Christ**
Chapter 1:24-2:5

Other books written by
Rebecca Herrington:


*777*
**Seals, Trumpets, Plagues:**
*A Gamble For Your Future*


**Devil's Storm**
*(Book One of The Storm Series)*

**Whirlwind of Evil**
*(Book Two of The Storm Series)*

**Cleansing Rain**
*(Book Three of The Storm Series)*

Coming soon...
**Winds of Reprieve**
*(Book Four of The Storm Series)*
**Hurricanes of Hell's Fury**
*(Book Five of The Storm Series)*


Thank you for reading my books. I would love to hear from you! You can contact me via the following email address:
Rebecca@HerringtonBooks.com


*May God richly bless you for your support of the ministry God has placed in my heart!*

*Rebecca*

www.ingramcontent.com/pod-product-compliance
Lightning Source LLC
Chambersburg PA
CBHW051741250726
48659CB00001B/179